MORRIS MINOR TRAVELLER

The Complete Companion

MORRIS MINOR TRAVELLER
The Complete Companion

By Ray Newell with Steve Foreman
Special Photography by John Colley

Herridge & Sons

Published in 2012 by
Herridge & Sons Ltd
Lower Forda,
Shebbear,
Beaworthy
Devon EX21 5SY

Reprinted 2015, 2021

Design by Ray Leaning, MUSE Fine Art & Design.
Special Photography by John Colley

© Copyright Ray Newell 2012

All rights reserved. No part of this publication may be reproduced in any form or by any means without the prior written permission of the publisher and the copyright holder.

ISBN 978-1-906133-45-0
Printed in China

CONTENTS

INTRODUCTION	6
CHAPTER 1	8
THE NEW POST-WAR MORRIS DESIGNS	
CHAPTER 2	18
MORRIS MINOR SERIES II TRAVELLER	
CHAPTER 3	32
MORRIS MINOR 1000 948cc TRAVELLER	
CHAPTER 4	44
MORRIS MINOR 1000 1098cc TRAVELLER	
CHAPTER 5	58
BUILDING THE TRAVELLER	
CHAPTER 6	66
DANISH SPECIAL: MORRIS 1000 COMBI	
CHAPTER 7	74
MILITARY AND POLICE TRAVELLERS	
CHAPTER 8	82
WOODWORK – DISMANTLING by Steve Foreman	
CHAPTER 9	98
WOODWORK – PREPARING AND FINISHING by Steve Foreman	
CHAPTER 10	101
WOODWORK – FITTING THE FRAME by Steve Foreman	
CHAPTER 11	118
WOODWORK – RESTORATION AND PARTIAL REPLACEMENT by Steve Foreman	
CHAPTER 12	122
TRAVELLER VARIATIONS	
CHAPTER 13	136
COMMERCIAL TRAVELLER CONVERSIONS	
CHAPTER 14	143
MODIFICATIONS AND UPGRADES	
APPENDIX - THE NUMBERS EXPLAINED:	153
ACKNOWLEDGMENTS	156

INTRODUCTION

The Minor always seems to have a smile on its face – and it will be bound to put a smile on your face too.

The post-war Morris Minor has become firmly established as an iconic British car. Designed by Alec Issigonis whose inspirational work resulted in the Morris Mini-Minor, better known the world over as the 'Mini', the whole Morris Minor range has had, and retains, a strong following, even from the time that the first vehicles rolled off the production lines in 1948. It became the first British car to reach the magical figure of one million in terms of production, and provided gainful employment for twenty-three years in Britain. CKD (Completely Knocked Down) models were assembled in sizeable numbers in many countries including Ireland, Holland, Denmark, South Africa, India, Australia, New Zealand, and the Philippines.

One of the most popular Morris Minors is the Traveller. Instantly recognisable, with its distinctive ash-framed body, the Traveller remains as popular today as it did during the eighteen years when it graced the showrooms of dealers around the world. Renowned for its versatility as a dual-purpose vehicle, the Traveller has secured its place in the hall of fame, so far as wood framed vehicles are concerned. The Morris Minor Traveller remained in production longer than any other 'Woodie' made anywhere, and was still selling well when it was phased out in 1971.

It has also been assigned many different 'titles' including being described by Dame Edna Everage as 'Shakespeare's car' when she spotted an example driving through Stratford, England. Though its origins do not go back quite that far, the term 'Shooting Brake' is another description applied to the Morris Minor Traveller. While never adopted officially, this term which was in common usage in the pre-war era to describe wood-framed 'utility' vehicles which were often used by shooting parties, continues to be used for the Traveller. When announced in 1953, BMC used the designation 'Station Wagon' for the new wood-framed model, no doubt influenced by the American practice which was current at the time. Later advertising material adopted 'Travellers' Car' as the preferred description, and this was finally refined to 'Traveller' as the official name.

The popularity of the Minor Traveller has continued throughout the post production era, and in recent years there has been renewed interest, as the virtues of the model have been recognised by a new generation of owners. For some,

A splendid example of the Series II model in its 1954-56 facelift version, with the unique 'Shooting Brake' (discussed in Chapter 12) in the background.

the pleasure of owning and maintaining an original specification vehicle from the 1950s, 1960s, or 1970s is sufficient. For others, the challenge of restoring a tired and worn-out Traveller and then enjoying the 'new' vehicle is even more satisfying. However, for an increasing number of owners upgrading the comfort and performance of their Traveller in order to make it a more useable vehicle in the twenty-first century has become a priority. Whatever your choice, the reassuring thing is that all the above are feasible.

The Morris Minor is one of those classic cars which have a large network of specialists who are able to supply replacement mechanical components, interior trim, and body panels to enable vehicles to be maintained, refurbished, restored, or upgraded. The ash frame, which incidentally is a structural part of the vehicle and subject to MOT regulations, can be replaced in part or in total. There is also a vibrant owners' club in the UK which provides help for members via a technical support service, as well as an informative bi-monthly magazine and web site. In most countries where the Morris Minor was exported to or built in significant numbers, there are Morris Minor Clubs which offer similar support.

For current or would-be Traveller owners, the pages which follow provide a useful insight into the development of the Traveller, the specifications of each of the models, and a detailed explanation of how to undertake a home-based project to replace all or some of the Traveller woodwork. There are also fascinating examples of rare and unusual Travellers, and a glimpse of what the future may hold, in terms of alternative mechanical upgrades and improved performance.

The Morris Minor Traveller has an illustrious past but it also has the potential to have a glorious future, given the infrastructure which exists to keep preserved examples on the road and return others to their former glory.

I would like to thank all who have helped with this book, but none more so than my co-author Steve Foreman and his son James of the Woodies company who have made a huge contribution, sharing the insights they have acquired from many years of working on Traveller restoration.

RAY NEWELL, May 2012

MORRIS MINOR TRAVELLER – THE COMPLETE COMPANION

CHAPTER 1
THE NEW POST-WAR MORRIS DESIGNS

THE NEW POST-WAR MORRIS DESIGNS

Morris Motors were at the forefront of automotive innovation with their new models which were introduced at the first post-war Motor Show held at Earls Court, London, in October 1948. Due in large part to the entrepreneurial skills of William Morris, by now Lord Nuffield, and the prodigious talents of Alec Issigonis, an up-and-coming car designer, Morris were able to launch a complete range of new cars. In the austere aftermath of World War Two, this was no mean achievement, and reflected considerable foresight and forward planning. As early as 1943, Government restrictions on developing new models had been relaxed sufficiently for Morris Motors to develop outline plans to produce a new range of vehicles featuring Small, Intermediate, and Large models.

Alec Issigonis was given the task of designing the all-new vehicles and he initially concentrated on the small car in the range. At first dubbed the Mosquito, this model eventually reached production as the Morris Minor Series MM. Marketed as the 'World's Supreme Small Car', it received universal acclaim for its monocoque body, flowing lines, and compact size. Initially two models were offered: a two-door saloon and an open tourer. Powered by the Morris Eight 918cc side-valve engine with a four-speed gearbox and floor change, the Minor featured independent front suspension with torsion bars, rack-and-pinion steering, and small 14in road wheels. The Minor represented a radical departure in UK small car design. Motoring journalists were quick to praise its appearance, comfort, vibrant colour and trim combinations, and most of all its driveability. The highly

effective suspension, superb handling, and overall economy of this compact vehicle placed the Minor well ahead of its rivals, and paved the way for a successful publicity campaign which established the Minor as a firm favourite with customers, both overseas and at home.

The basic design of the Minor was scaled up for the proposed Intermediate model which was launched at the same time, as the Morris Oxford Series MO. This mid-range model was offered as a four-door saloon and much was expected of it. Morris Motors had hopes that the Oxford would be the export flagship of the new range. Extensive

The all-new Morris Minor – highly acclaimed and the undoubted star of the Earls Court Motor Show when it made its debut.

Features of the new design included monocoque construction, independent adjustable torsion bar springing, and rack-and-pinion steering.

Alec Issigonis: the inspiration behind the post-war range of Morris Cars announced in 1948.

The first of the Minors, the Series MM model, with its headlights set low in the grille. It was introduced in 1948 as a two-door saloon, with four doors an option from 1951, before being replaced by the Series II in 1952.

The Morris Oxford Series MO was marketed as the 'Car motorists in every land have asked for' – a clear statement of the expectation that it would be successful in overseas markets.

The Morris Oxford retained many of the features of its smaller companion but differed in the use of column gear change, a bench-type front seat, and by being available with four doors from the beginning of production.

consultations were undertaken across the world-wide dealer network, to ascertain what would be the key features of their ideal car design. In subsequent advertising, Morris claimed that the new Oxford was 'The car motorists in every land have asked for'.

In terms of body styling, the Oxford shared many of the features of the original Mosquito prototype, albeit on a larger scale. However, the front end was significantly different, with many pundits alleging that Issigonis was heavily influenced by American designs. Certainly the large front grille was reminiscent of those used on some transatlantic models. In other respects, the Oxford remained true to the characteristic features of the Minor MM. Like its smaller counterpart, the Oxford MO had a monocoque body, independent front suspension with torsion bars, and rack-and-pinion steering. There were still sufficient differences for the road tester from *The Motor* to claim without hesitation that it was 'a new car from end to end'. The interior was roomy with a bench-type front seat, column gear

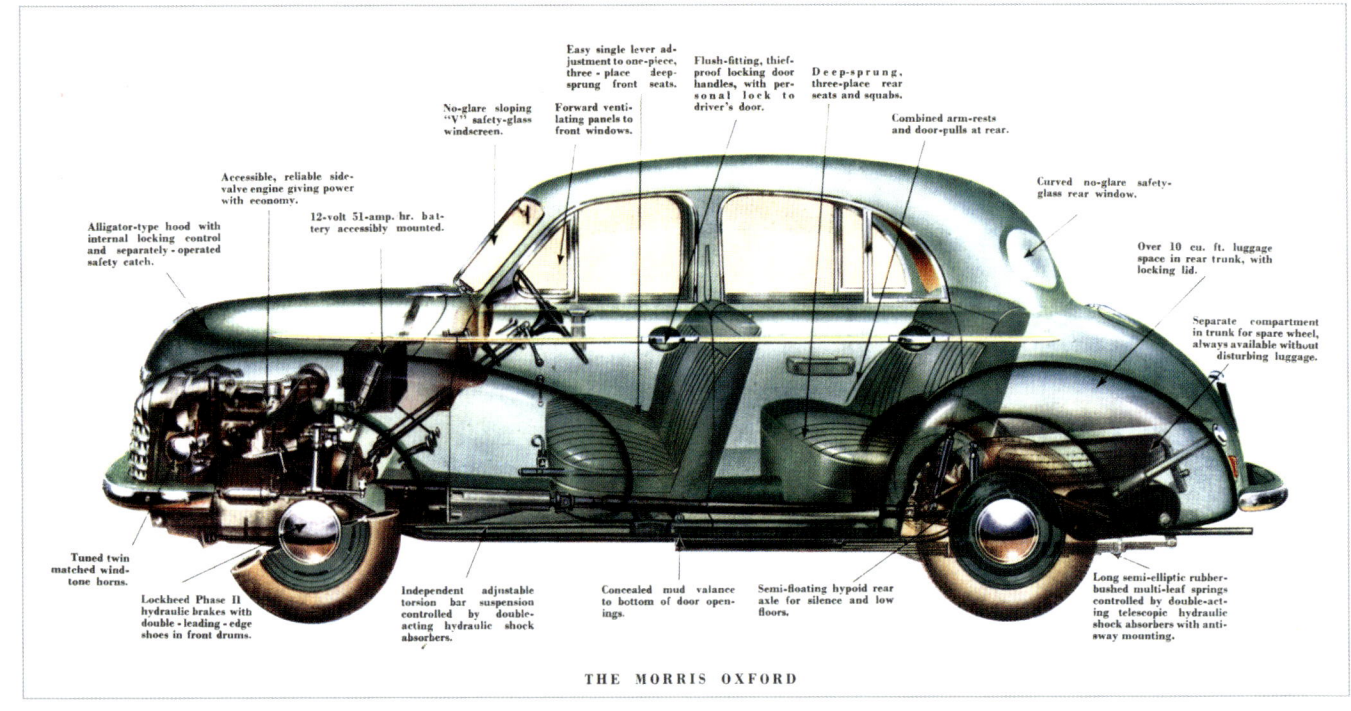

change, and a well laid out dashboard with clear instrumentation and easily reached controls. The four-door body allowed easy access to the rear seat, where there was ample space for three adults to sit in comfort.

Mechanically, the new 1476cc short-stroke (73.5mm by 87mm) four-cylinder, side-valve engine was designed to develop proportionately more power at low speeds in relation to its maximum output at peak revolutions. This provided maximum torque to aid top gear acceleration, and proved more than adequate for the different demands made of it around the world. Like the new Minor, the Oxford was well received by the motoring journalists in 1948. While acknowledging the 'family likeness' the Morris Oxford was recognised for its own distinctive characteristics, and praised as being a very attractive vehicle which was pleasant to handle on the road. Compliments abounded about the positive steering, smooth gear change, excellent suspension, and flexible top gear performance. With such plaudits, it is not surprising that the order book for the new Morris Oxford quickly filled up, with export markets taking priority.

The final model in the line-up was the Morris Six Series MS which allowed Morris Motors to meet its objective of having a new large car at the Motor Show. However, the Six only just made it to the show, and work on its development continued for some considerable time after the official launch. In fact, it was March 1949 before production began in earnest. Lord Nuffield had a significant influence on the design and styling of this model. He had already shown an aversion to the design of the prototype Mosquito by famously referring to it as 'looking like a poached egg'. Incidentally, he also had the final say in naming the new small car the Morris Minor, after its ancestor of twenty years before. In a similar vein, he decreed that the Six should have an upright grille reminiscent of Morris pre-war designs, and be powered by a six-cylinder overhead-valve engine.

In styling terms, from the bulkhead back the Morris Six was similar to the Oxford, only the front doors being different. Both Jack Daniels and Reg Job who had been close associates of Alec Issigonis, and were responsible for overseeing many aspects of the design of the Morris Minor, recalled in their later years that a simple overlay technique had been used to design the Six. Using the Oxford as a template, the new front end for the Six was simply added on. While this was fine in principle and looked good on the draughtsman's drawing board, in practice it was a completely different story.

The six-cylinder 2214cc engine (73.5mm by 87mm, as the Oxford) had a single overhead camshaft, and was perhaps based on the Hispano-Suiza aero engine which had inspired many pre-war Wolseleys and MGs. It suited Issigonis, as it complied with the nose-heavy design principle that he favoured. However, fitting this weighty engine in an extended front end added to the Oxford monocoque body presented a

The Morris Six MS, on Lord Nuffield's insistence, retained the use of an upright radiator grille, more reminiscent of pre-war cars.

The three models – Minor, Oxford and Six – were often promoted together in publicity material.

MORRIS MINOR TRAVELLER – THE COMPLETE COMPANION

By 1952, the 'Quality First' slogan had made its appearance in Morris publicity.

With a late-model Minor saloon in the foreground, the Traveller versions of the Minor and the more imposing Series MO Oxford make an interesting contrast.

multitude of challenges. Structural problems arose under test with evidence of metal fatigue, particularly in the bulkhead area near the longitudinal chassis legs, and around the shock absorber mounting points. Extensive testing under the guidance of Charles Griffin, Chief Experimental Engineer, eventually resulted in additional strengthening being added in both areas, and the use of improved telescopic shock absorbers.

With further improvements made to the steering geometry, the Morris Six entered full production. It sold moderately well, but home market sales were eclipsed by exports. Out of a total of 12,186 cars made, only 5028 were home market sales. However, in a shrewd marketing ploy and to rationalise the Nuffield range, the basic design of the Morris Six was adopted for the Wolseley 6/80. With improved trim and slightly better performance, courtesy of twin carburettors, this up-market model reached a more respectable sales total. A shorter wheelbase model, the Wolseley 4/50, was added to the range, fitted with a four-cylinder version of the ohc engine.

ONGOING DEVELOPMENTS

No sooner had the Morris Minor entered production, than Alec Issigonis was forced back to the drawing board. Morris had high hopes that the Minor would sell well in North America. However, the low position of the headlamps on the Minor Series MM fell foul of the lighting regulations in the state of California. Consequently, an urgent rethink on the front-end design of the highly regarded Morris Minor was needed. The result was a changed profile to the front wings (fenders), to fit the headlamps in a higher position. Even though Issigonis was reluctant to accept the change, on the basis that it detracted from the aerodynamic look of the original design and reduced the top speed by one mile per hour, the enforced change became one of the trademark features of the Morris Minor. Initially, sales of the high headlamp models were restricted to overseas markets, but in 1950 all Series MM Minors adopted this arrangement, and with it changes to the front valance, side lights, and bumpers.

By 1949, attention was turning to expanding the Minor range. Prototype models of a four-door saloon had already been produced and the draughtsmen, no doubt aided by the work already done on the Oxford Series MO four-door saloon, were hard at work determining what revisions would be needed to the monocoque shell to incorporate two extra doors. The key changes required were to move the B-posts forward and shorten the front doors.

When the model was launched at the 1950 London Motor Show, the opportunity was taken to promote the four-door saloon as a higher specification model. Unfortunately for home market customers, many of whom were still suffering the effects of World War Two rationing, the four-door saloon was at first only available to overseas customers.

THE NEW POST-WAR MORRIS DESIGNS

The 'Export or Die' rallying cry had the desired effect, as overseas sales soared to unexpected levels. Morris Motors enjoyed buoyant sales figures for all their new post-war models. A new facility was built at Cowley in order to supply the growing number of overseas plants wanting to assemble Morris cars from CKD (Completely Knocked Down) kits.

Work continued apace in the Experimental Department at Cowley, as attention turned again to expanding the range of Morris models. With developments already in hand on the Morris Minor, attention switched to the Oxford Series MO. Plans included developing light commercial variants based on the cab and mechanical components of the saloon model, and a Utilicon vehicle with rear side windows. Issigonis initiated the original design plans for all of these vehicles. The light commercial vehicles took precedence and by 1950, 10cwt (500kg) van and pick-up variants were ready for full-scale production. Powered by the same 1476cc side-valve engine as used in the saloon models and with most of the same mechanical features, these commercial vehicles were marketed as Morris Cowley half-ton vans and pick-ups, series MCV. Both variants proved popular, with the van being singled out for considerable praise in the motoring press due to its impressive 120 cu.ft (3.24 cubic metres) load capacity, and the ease of access through the wide-opening rear doors.

In the case of the vehicle referred to by the Experimental Department as the Utilicon, this was in fact a Traveller. Reference has already been made to the impact of transatlantic influences on Alec Issigonis's styling. The popularity of the American 'station wagon' with its wooden sides or wood panelling no doubt played its part, when his thoughts turned to producing a wood-framed multi-purpose utility vehicle. Experimental work on the Morris Oxford Series MO Traveller began in 1951. In the same year, work also started on a prototype Morris Minor version.

THE MORRIS OXFORD MO TRAVELLERS' CAR

It was widely thought that any development work on a Morris Oxford based 'Station Wagon' or 'Traveller' would have begun by using a separate chassis, similar to that used on the MCV vehicle. Jack Daniels, Issigonis's second-in-command, who had a high regard for the Morris Oxford, confirmed some years ago that in fact some experimentation with a short chassis, married to the Oxford cab, was considered in order to provide additional strength, rigidity, and load-bearing capacity for the prototype Oxford-based Utilicon. The plan was to mount a wood frame – with either wood or metal inserts – on this structure in order to create a sturdy and functional dual-purpose vehicle which would have an appeal in overseas markets, particularly in America.

On the prototype vehicle, plywood panels were inserted into an ash frame, for the body as well as the rear doors. Development work on the wood frame was undertaken at the

The Morris Oxford Travellers' Car prototype. Ongoing developments can be seen when comparing these two photographs. Note use of wooden side panels, difference in the shape and thickness of the ash frame, arrangements for semaphore indicators, and the change from painted to stainless steel front window frames.

The early brochure for the Morris Oxford Travellers' Car shows the original grille as found on Saloons until 1952. Only a few Travellers' Cars were produced with this grille.

A popular and versatile 10cwt commercial based on the Oxford MO was produced in van and pick-up form. Both featured a separate chasis.

Morris Bodies Plant in Coventry, with subsequent testing and final appraisal taking place in the Experimental Department at Cowley. Keeping the weight of the proposed new vehicle as low as possible was a priority. With an extended roof line, a large expanse of glass, and the larger metal side panels to contend with, care needed to be taken to minimise the risk of excessive weight or unbalanced weight distribution, which could adversely affect the handling and overall performance of the new vehicle. In an effort to keep the weight to a minimum, the separate chassis frame idea was eventually dropped in favour of using a slightly modified version of the Oxford saloon cab and monocoque floorpan. The use of aluminium inserts for the side panels, the rear doors, and the roof panel, helped bring about some further weight reduction.

The prototype used the 1476cc side valve engine and virtually all of the mechanical components, as found in the saloon and light commercial models. Like the commercial vehicles, the rear springs used were the nine-leaf type. The large mazak front grille from the saloon and the Morris Cowley vans and pick-ups was also incorporated, presumably to save on costs, and to add an element of consistency across the range.

PRODUCTION MODELS

The Morris Oxford Travellers' Car entered production in October 1952. It was particularly well received in the motoring press. *The Autocar* described it as 'A very attractive all purpose vehicle' stating that 'it is smart, has very pleasing lines, and gives satisfactory performance. It is quite economical on fuel and has particularly good carrying capacity.' Many features came in for positive comment, including overall performance and road holding. The side-valve engine was described as being quiet and smooth in operation, with good power at low speed. While recognising that the vehicle was designed with the emphasis on load carrying rather than speed, much was made of the stability of the vehicle, and it was pointed out that the Travellers' Car could be cornered quite quickly, whatever the load, with very little roll.

All-round visibility was deemed to be excellent, so much so that a somewhat exuberant road tester described riding in the rear seat as having 'almost a feeling of riding in an open car with the hood down, with the added comfort, on a cold winter's day, of the warmth provided by a very satisfactory heating system.' Naturally the storage capacity warranted special attention, and the ease with which the rear seat could be stowed to provide additional loading capacity was

THE NEW POST-WAR MORRIS DESIGNS

praised. However, one note of constructive criticism did emerge, with regard to the exposed painted rear wheel arches and the lack of covering on the rear floor area of the load compartment. It was felt that the overall appearance would have been improved, if these areas had been lined.

EARLY CHANGES

Though a few of the earliest production models, including the one provided for road test purposes featured the mazak front grille, this was soon dropped in favour of a much more flamboyant stainless steel fabricated version, more akin to those which featured on many American cars of the early 1950s. This dramatically changed the frontal appearance of the saloon and Travellers' Car models; the Cowley commercial vehicles kept the original grille. Its use on the Travellers' Car, combined with publicity which described the vehicle as a 'Station Wagon', was no doubt aimed at the American market. Though it did prove popular in overseas markets with exports outstripping home market sales, the total number of Morris Oxford MO Travellers' Cars produced reached only a modest 5550. However, developments at boardroom level which were destined to have significant impact on future models were looming large, with the merger between Austin and the Nuffield Organization in 1952. The Series MO was replaced by the Morris Oxford Series II model in 1954, with in effect an Austin engine under the bonnet. The Traveller version of the Series II had a steel body, but still featured timber trim. The Morris Isis and the short-lived Oxford Series III Traveller also used this hybrid body, until Morris introduced the Oxford Series IV all-steel four-door Traveller in August 1957.

Ian Biltcliffe's Morris Oxford MO Travellers' Car retains many original features.

MORRIS MINOR TRAVELLER – THE COMPLETE COMPANION

Wide opening rear doors made for easy loading. The rear end styling was simple and functional.

The rear load area, which when the rear seat was folded down offered oceans of storage space, made the MO Travellers' Car a popular choice for travelling salesmen.

The 1476cc side-valve engine fitted to the Morris Oxford Travellers' Car was praised by road testers who found it to be smooth and flexible in operation.

THE NEW POST-WAR MORRIS DESIGNS

Bench type front seats, column gear change and ratchet-type handbrake were all features of the MO Oxford range. The Travellers' Car's front bench seat had a divided backrest, which hinged forward to provide access to the rear compartment. Moulded rubber floor covering was standard equipment.

The rear bench seat was deemed adequate for three people. The additional small table installation is a non-standard item but a nice touch.

CHAPTER 2
MINOR SERIES II TRAVELLER

SERIES II TRAVELLER

While work was progressing on the Morris Oxford Series MO Traveller in readiness for launch as a production model, elsewhere in the Experimental Department at Cowley attention turned to producing a smaller version, based on the Morris Minor. Much more is known about the initial ideas for the proposed new model, as one of the early prototype vehicles was released for sale from the factory and passed into private ownership. Experimental model EX/SMM/180 was, according to factory records, a Morris Minor Utilicon. Built in March 1951, it used the 'short bonnet' arrangement common to the Morris Minor of that era, and was powered by the Series MM 918cc side-valve engine.

Though Alec Issigonis had a considerable influence on the new model, the draughtsman responsible for much of the work was Eric Carter. The experimental model had a number of interesting features which suggest that not all the elements of the design of the Oxford Series MO Traveller (which was well advanced) were automatically going to be incorporated into the smaller model. The absence of a steel B-post on either side of the vehicle, while an interesting concept, no doubt compromised rigidity and was soon dropped. Similarly the inclusion of a full-length fabric roof panel, flanked by metal side panels attached to the front screen cowling, presumably in an effort to reduce the overall weight of the vehicle, was an idea not pursued on eventual production models. Other experimental features such as a falling line to the top of the rear side windows, slightly differently-shaped rear doors, and the lack of rear bumpers, were all changed before it was decided to put this model into production.

Somewhat surprisingly EX/SMM/180 was released from the Experimental Department in August 1952 and was sold as a used vehicle. It was registered as SJO 133 and remained in use for many years. (See the sidebar for the history of this vehicle.) At this stage interest in producing a Traveller version of the Morris Minor seems to have waned, as it was not until April 1953 that another experimental model was produced. Featuring the BMC A-series 803cc overhead valve engine, EX/FLE11/214 was listed in the experimental records as a Travellers' Car. More extensive development work was completed on this particular vehicle, including rigorous testing at Chalgrove Aerodrome and on the *pavé* surface at the MIRA proving ground, where in the words of Peter Tothill, who worked in the Experimental Department, 'the vehicle rigidity was compromised by the ash frame'. The vehicle in question survived the ordeal and was repainted and renumbered in 1954, after production of the Morris Minor 'Station Wagon' had begun.

PPX 344 is one of the earliest surviving Series II Travellers.

EX/SMM/180: THE PROTOTYPE

When released from the Experimental Department in 1952, this vehicle which was designated as a Utilicon, was sold to Mrs C Kingerlee, wife of the Company Secretary of Morris Motors Ltd. It remained in family ownership until 1963 when it was sold by Morris Garages of Oxford. The new owner, Mr T Robertson, whose wife was the daughter of Mr Jack Lownes, the then works manager of MG at Abingdon, had the vehicle for two years, before passing it on to his father, the Reverend TE Robertson. On his retirement from the ministry, he took the vehicle to Edinburgh, Scotland. By all accounts it provided sound, reliable transport until 1969, when problems with the rear axle forced it off the road. Efforts to secure a home for what was known to be a vehicle of historic significance in a motor museum failed, and it was eventually sold to someone in Perthshire. Regrettably there is no record of the vehicle having survived, but what is known about it provides a useful insight into the development of the Morris Minor Traveller.

An exceptionally rare photograph of the prototype Utilicon EX/SMM/180, showing many unique features including an early front cab with a 'short' Series MM bonnet, a full length vinyl roof and sloping side windows.

THE MORRIS MINOR SERIES II

Ongoing work on the next phase of the development of the Morris Minor was focussed on a suitable replacement for the 918cc engine used in the Series MM models. By 1951, consideration was being given to using an engine based on the 918cc side-valve engine, but with pushrod-operated overhead valves, which had been developed for use in the Wolseley Eight in 1939. The Wolseley Eight only went into production in 1946 and was discontinued in 1948, but the ohv engine remained on the stocks, and no fewer than six prototype Morris Minors were fitted with this engine and prepared for final testing.

MORRIS MINOR TRAVELLER – THE COMPLETE COMPANION

The much vaunted 803cc engine offered increased power, improved performance, and better acceleration than previous sidevalve-powered Morris Minors.

In November 1951, The Nuffield Organization, of which Morris Motors Ltd was the most significant part, and the Austin Motor Company Ltd, announced that they were to merge to form the British Motor Corporation Ltd (BMC). In the process they formed the fourth biggest motor manufacturing company in the world. In spite of the merger, bitter rivalries continued, none more so than when it was announced in October 1952 that the Morris Minor would be fitted with the overhead-valve 803cc A-series engine, as used in the baby Austin A30 saloon which had been launched a year earlier. In purely commercial terms it made sense, but there was a lot of disquiet in the Morris ranks about the Austin engine's capability and its suitability for use in the heavier Morris Minor.

Hopes were high that this engine would transform the Morris Minor in terms of performance, given its power output of 33bhp at 4400rpm. However, developments at boardroom level were destined to quell any such optimism, much to the annoyance of Jack Daniels, who rated the Wolseley engine very highly, having driven a Minor fitted with one quite extensively.

The die was cast for the next phase of the Minor's development and for a time, while Minor Series MM production continued, the Austin engine was fitted to Minor four-door saloons. When Series MM production came to an end in February 1953, all Minors were re-designated as Series II models. Two-door saloons, four-door saloons, and tourers continued in production, with light commercial vehicles in the form of the quarter-ton or O-type Morris Minor van and pick-up being added to the model range in May 1953. All of these vehicles used the A-series engine and the corresponding gearbox, and a new BMC rear axle was soon added, being first used on the Traveller which had it from the start of production.

LAUNCH OF THE MINOR TRAVELLER

In October 1953, the Morris Minor Station Wagon, later to be called the Travellers' Car, was announced to an expectant public at the London Motor Show. Like the rest of the Series II Minors on the stand, it was powered by the 803cc A-series engine. From the outset the 'Traveller' as it was to become known, was offered in standard and De Luxe specifications. The De Luxe model had carpet on the wheel arches in the front footwells, leather on the front seat facings, front bumper over riders, a heater, and a second sun visor for the front passenger. A rubber mat for the rear load compartment was soon added on De Luxe models.

The Traveller shared most of the design features of the rest of the Series II range, particularly the front end styling up to the B-post, fascia, instrumentation, interior trim, and mechanical components, but had seven-leaf rather than five-leaf rear springs. On the saloon and tourer models, the only external difference between a Series MM model and a Series II was the changed bonnet motif. By contrast, the Station Wagon stood out as a new and exciting addition to the range.

The original designation for what was to become known as The Traveller was the 'Station Wagon'. This was no doubt influenced by the American custom of calling panelled estate cars Station Wagons.

SERIES II TRAVELLER

The clean-cut lines of the ash frame and the original front end design of the Series II models, inherited from the Series MM, are clearly shown in these photographs of a pre-production car. The internal shot shows an interesting contrast in the front and rear seat trim patterns.

With its distinctive ash frame, painted aluminium side and rear door panels, and redesigned detachable rear wings, the vehicle looked imposing and elicited favourable comments and comparisons to some of the British pre-war wood-framed shooting brakes. When viewed with the rear doors open and the rear seat stowed, to reveal the capacious load area of 50in by 38in (127cm by 97cm), its potential for use as a dual-purpose vehicle was immediately apparent. When driven, the excellent features of the rest of the range, in terms of steering, suspension and handling which were already well proven, were reassuringly just the same.

Interior appointments were also the same, with the instrument panel in front of the driver, featuring a cream-faced speedometer flanked by separate gauges for petrol and oil pressure. In the centre of the dash was a grille with an ash tray built in, and simple switch gear below. The front passenger had a glove box with a Morris motif on the lid, and a parcel shelf below the dash offered additional storage. Pre-production Travellers had the original Minor-type front seats with transverse panels, but the rear seat and soon also the front seats had a new pattern of narrow longitudinal flutes, in groups of five.

MORRIS MINOR TRAVELLER – THE COMPLETE COMPANION

Joint advertising illustrating the family likeness between the Morris Oxford Series MO and the Morris Minor, both of which were re designated as Travellers' Car.

Features of the Early Series II models included the retention of the Series MM style fascia (right) with gold-coloured instrument panel and glove box lid, replaced by the facelift fascia (above) in 1954.

SERIES II TRAVELLER

well-finished vehicle with van capacity but car comfort and performance.

4. Perfect balance—wheelbase, height and track are proportioned correctly.

5. Attractive, freshly styled radiator grille greatly improves frontal appearance.

B THE FRONT

1. Torsion bar independent front suspension permits exceptionally good road-holding and cornering with the most comfortable "ride."

2. Hydraulic piston-type shock absorbers keep the ride smooth.

3. Separate sidelights and double-dipping-type headlights.

4. 12-volt lighting and ignition system.

5. Rack-and-pinion steering. Very light to handle and extremely accurate—good point with ladies.

6. O.H.V. engine gives good cruising and top-gear performance with good acceleration and hill climbing.

7. S.U. fuel pump and carburetter.

8. Bonnet released from inside car. Double safety-catch at front.

9. Engine accessibility good; easy access for routine servicing and maintenance.

10. Good mileage per gallon. Low overall running costs. Favourable power/weight ratio.

11. Lockheed hydraulic brakes on all four wheels. Easily adjustable.

C FOR DRIVER & FRONT SEAT PASSENGER

1. Re-styled facia includes two spacious glove trays. Instruments incorporated in one large easily read dial, which is conveniently situated, with the controls, in the centre of the panel.

2. Full-width parcel tray under facia.

3. Ventilating panels in door windows open out to act as air scoops in really hot weather.

4. Driver's sun visor securely retained by friction mounting in required position. Passenger's sun visor in De-luxe model.

5. Both front seats hinge forward independently for access to rear compartment.

6. Door hinges are concealed. Outside front door handles are flush-fitting, pull-out type.

7. Instrument light indicates when sidelights are on.

8. Twin blade electric windscreen wiper.

9. Four-speed gearbox. Gear lever in central position. Positive in action with synchromesh on second, third and fourth gears.

10. Hand brake operates by cable on rear wheels.

11. Front door windows wind fully down.

12. Forward hinged doors have double-action safety lock—good point with parents of young children.

13. Trafficator switch. Flashing direction indicators on all LHD models.

14. Radio easily installed.

15. Adjustable bucket-type front seat for driver.

16. Easy car to drive. Small turning circle, compact overall size allow easy parking, garaging and excellent manoeuvrability in traffic.

17. Good driving vision. Slender corner and door pillars eliminate blind spots.

18. Fitted rubber mats for long life and easy cleaning.

19. Sprung steering wheel with horn button in centre.

20. Foot-operated headlamp dipping switch, leaving hands free.

D FOR REAR SEAT PASSENGERS

1. Rear seat is forward of rear axle.

2. Hypoid rear axle for quiet operation and long life.

3. Ample elbow, leg and head room for passengers.

4. By folding the rear seat the vehicle's luggage carrying capacity is greatly increased. Even when carrying four passengers, there is still plenty of room for luggage and equipment behind the rear seat.

5. Large side windows with sliding panels give excellent vision and adequate ventilation. Safety glass all round.

6. The roof lining panels are covered in washable leathercloth. Central roof light.

7. Extra sturdy long semi-elliptic rear springs, with rubber mountings—piston-type hydraulic shock absorbers.

To ensure none of the innovative features of the Traveller were missed, a comprehensive 'Walk Around Sales Guide' was provided for salesmen.

The absence of bumper overriders indicates that this model is a 'Standard' model.

Changes such as they were, were noted but remained understated. The fact that the new vehicle was only one inch longer than the saloon came as a surprise to many. So too did the extent of the storage capacity which, at its maximum, totalled 33 cu.ft (891 litres). Improvements in performance, courtesy of the new engine with power now increased to 30bhp, which offered quicker acceleration and a higher top speed of 65mph (105km/h), were all promoted as positive indicators of progress.

Understandably all these features were highlighted and reinforced in contemporary advertising, which soon picked up on the potential for marketing the already well-established Morris Oxford Series MO Traveller alongside the new Minor model, as Travellers' Cars. The potential for use as a commercial vehicle was also stressed. Given the circumstances of the time, when travelling salesmen plied their trade door-to-door, the Travellers' Car was promoted as being ideal, both for business purposes and for family transport.

Reaction in the motoring press to the Morris Minor Station Wagon was reassuringly good and boded well for future sales. The fact that the Travellers' Car was trimmed to saloon car standards and was available in either standard or De

The new radiator grille seen here arrived on the Series II in 1954, and the side lamps moved to the wings, but the split windscreen remained for another two years.

Luxe specifications was recognised as providing a welcome choice to discerning customers. The capacity for carrying up to 4cwt (200kg) in the load area behind the front seat was favourably commented on, as was the ease with which goods were loaded, thanks to the wide opening rear doors which could be securely locked in the open position. On reviewing the Travellers' Car in 1953, *The Motor* concluded that 'Well known for economy and good handling qualities, the Minor will win new admirers with this body, which is to sell at a basic price of £422 10s.' With British Purchase Tax added (at the time, 50 per cent of the wholesale price), the total price for a standard specification Travellers' Car was £599 13s4d. De Luxe specification models were priced at £622 6s8d including Purchase Tax.

LATER SERIES II UPDATES
Within a year of the Travellers' Car being introduced, some 'minor' styling changes were announced for the whole of the Minor range in October 1954. These were mainly confined to the front end arrangement, and the internal dash and fascia panel. Even though it had only been in production for a short time, the Travellers' Car was updated at the same time. The most obvious change was the new radiator grille with individual painted horizontal slats and a chrome surround, rather than the one-piece 'cheese-grater' grille fitted to the Series MM and early Series II models. The grille surround panel was different too, as it no longer housed the side lights. On the updated models, these were moved to a new position on the front wings below the headlamps.

Internally, the most striking change was the introduction of a larger, centrally-positioned speedometer which housed warning lights for ignition, oil pressure, headlamp main beam, and water temperature (or, on some models, indicators). It also incorporated the fuel gauge. Open glove boxes either side created a much more modern look, as well as an impression of spaciousness. Elsewhere in the interior there were other changes. The front seat frames were slightly modified and fitted with a stronger base. The same trim colours were offered, and the fluted pattern for the seat upholstery was now used also on saloon and tourer models. The mechanical specification was unchanged. In spite of the updates to the Travellers' Car, the retail price was not increased. Sales, both at home and abroad, were promising, but the first signs of the limitations of the engine and gearbox were emerging in road test reports, particularly in America.

When *The Motor* road tested a De Luxe model Travellers' Car in 1955, as one might have anticipated, there were encouraging remarks about the general design, layout, and handling of the vehicle. The versatility of the vehicle was unquestioned. However, certain aspects came in for constructive criticism and others for more barbed remarks. Visibility was described as generally excellent, but was limited in some respects, most notably towards the front where the thick windscreen pillars occasionally obscured forward vision. The fact that it was impossible to see the nearside front wing from the driving seat was also noted. So too was the suitability of the driving position, as evidenced from the following extract: 'As with the majority of recent Morris models, the small steering wheel has comparatively little rake [they probably meant the column had little rake], with the engine and driving seat being positioned well forward in the car. The seat squab in this case is too upright for the majority of tastes, suiting those of small stature better than those of average height or tall men.' Another small niggle was that the recently-introduced open glove lockers or cubby holes were devoid of any lip, to prevent their contents being spilled under acceleration!

Of more serious concern was the assessment of overall performance from the 803cc engine and gearbox. The following succinct summary makes for interesting reading even though it was written over half a century ago: 'Unexpectedly the Traveller, as an alternative version of the well liked Minor, may not appeal *per se* to every partisan of that car. Economical and able to cruise surprisingly fast, the Utility lacks something of the air of what could only be described as eagerness in the slightly lighter saloons, and though its response to the controls is quick and positive, a

Performance with the 803cc ohv engine was reasonably brisk and well up to the standard of other small cars of the time, while the Minor was more sure-footed on the road than most contemporary competitors.

MORRIS MINOR TRAVELLER – THE COMPLETE COMPANION

Forward tipping passenger seat allowed easy access to comfortable rear seats.

little of the surefootedness is missing'. The reason was immediately identified: 'It is emphatically not a car which asks to be hurried, a state of affairs for which a rather fussy, wide-ratio gearbox is partly responsible'. While praising the engine for its flexibility and ability to maintain prolonged high speeds, concern was raised once again about the gear change: 'For overtaking or for attacks on lengthy hills a change down from top to third is possible up to a speed of about 40mph, but the practice of gear changing in general is discouraged by the widely spaced ratios and by "sticky" synchromesh which is very easily beaten.'

The concerns expressed here were unfortunately repeated elsewhere. In America where there were high hopes for sales of the pocket-sized Travellers' Car or, as Americans called it, Station Wagon, even harsher judgements were passed, occasionally in very brash terms. Tom Cahill writing for *Mechanix Illustrated* was not impressed with the power output from the 803cc engine, noting rather disparagingly that it needed a bit more 'oomph' in order to 'beat the junkman's horse away from a traffic light'. While this may have been a bit unkind, it did highlight the fact that in spite of all the plaudits about the Traveller's handling, economy and versatility, the average American customer would be bound to expect a higher level of performance than was

Changed dash layout with central speedometer characterised the 1954 update.

available from this compact British 'Woodie'.

Elsewhere in the States even the effusive Editor of *Auto Age*, who picked up a brand new early Series II Station Wagon from the JS Inskip showroom in New York for a weekend test, had some reservations. With only 23 miles on the clock, caution had to be exercised to run the vehicle in. Nevertheless, in spite of the praise heaped on the Station Wagon for its positive steering, ease of handling, and impressive suspension, he still found occasion to quibble over the gearbox. In spite of claiming that the Station Wagon went up and down and around corners like a roller coaster gone wild, drifting just enough wherever necessary, with little more than a hint and a nudge from him, his assessment of the gearbox was decidedly less positive: 'The thing that bothered me was the gearbox [or as it would normally be called in America, the transmission]... In fact the synchromesh is real good and the gearbox is one of the easiest and fastest shifting ones you'll come across. It's just that I don't happen to like the choice of gear ratios; first is too low, and third does not have enough speed on it. I'm told that with the engine really broken in correctly that you can squeeze 49mph (79 km/h) out of the thing in third, but even that is sort of slow.'

In the final analysis, Harvey B Janes did praise the Minor Station Wagon, even if not everyone would agree with his conclusion: 'If you are looking for a buggy that's fun to drive and safe and can carry vast amounts of groceries, hardware, luggage or what have you, then it's something to consider seriously. It's not terribly fast... on the other hand that gas economy is nothing to sneer at, and the Morris Station Wagon does hold more luggage than any small car I've ever seen – actually more than our big sedans. Its space is usable too and plenty easy to get at with those pick-up truck rear doors. It seems to me that in view of the easy handling, light steering and good positive brakes that this is just a perfect car for a woman. For shopping in and around town, parking in small spaces or winding along country lanes it cannot be beaten.'

Though some may baulk at these comments today, the reality was that the Morris Minor models, including the Station Wagon, were purchased by many Americans as second cars. However by 1955, sales in America, so far the long hoped-for boom export market, were on the slide, even though total Series II sales world-wide showed a continuing upward trend. Less than glowing press comments coupled with feedback from dealerships at home and abroad highlighted some of the shortcomings of the Series II, and indicated that the Morris Minor was in need of a new lease of life, if the overall increase in sales was to continue.

The simple tail lamp, with reflector above.

Easy access to the load area was offered by wide opening rear doors.

One of the major selling points for the Travellers' Car was the substantial storage area on offer when the rear seats were folded forward.

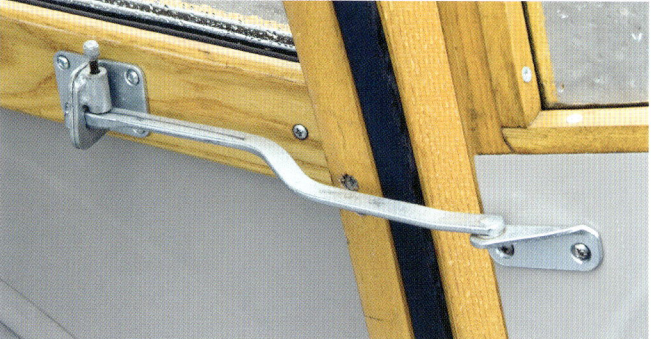

The stay that holds the rear door in the open position.

TOOL KIT

The Series II Travellers' Car had a comprehensive tool kit as standard equipment. It contained the following items which were supplied in a plastic tool roll: jack, wheel brace, tyre pump, grease gun, distributor gauge and screwdriver, drain plug key, tommy bar, three open-ended spanners, one box spanner, and one screwdriver.

SERIES II TRAVELLER

Nowadays the semaphore indicators or trafficators are a talking point if preserved in working order.

Plain rear door panels were a feature of the Series II Travellers car. The closed/locked door handle position shown here is correct for this model.

MORRIS MINOR TRAVELLER – THE COMPLETE COMPANION

The Minor engine bay is wide and spacious, and the small engine is nearly dwarfed by ancillaries. This is the 803cc unit.

The difference beteen the frontal arrangement on the early and late Series II Travellers is clearly illustrated here.

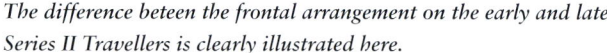

SERIES II TRAVELLER

MINOR SERIES II TRAVELLER SPECIFICATION 1953-56

ENGINE
Cast-iron block and head, pressed steel sump, four cylinders in line, pushrod operated overhead valves
Bore and stroke: 58mm x 76mm; capacity: 803cc
Compression ratio: 7:2:1
Maximum power: 30bhp at 4800rpm
Maximum torque: 40lb/ft at 2400rpm
Fuel pump: SU type L
Carburettor: SU type HS1
Air cleaner: dry gauze type

TRANSMISSION
Front engine, rear wheel drive. Four speed gearbox in unit with engine. Synchromesh on second, third, and top gears. Centre floor gear change.
Clutch: Borg and Beck single dry plate 6¼in (157mm)
Gear ratios: first 4.09:1; second 2.588:1; third 1.679:1; top.1.000:1; reverse 5.180:1
Final drive: hypoid bevel three-quarter floating axle with banjo casing; ratio 5.286:1 or 7:37
Overall ratios: first 21.618:1; second 13.69:1; third 8.88:1; top 5.286:1; reverse 27.38:1

SUSPENSION
Front: independent by torsion bars and links, lever-arm hydraulic shock absorbers
Rear: half elliptic seven-leaf springs, lever-arm hydraulic shock absorbers

BRAKES
Lockheed hydraulic, 7in drums (178mm)
Front: two leading shoes; rear: one leading and one trailing shoe

STEERING
Rack and pinion, 2½ turns lock to lock; turning circle 33ft (10m)

WHEELS AND TYRES
Wheels: 14in pressed steel disc with four bolt fixing; tyres 5.00 x 14

DIMENSIONS AND WEIGHT
Wheelbase: 7ft 2in (218.4cm)
Track: front 4ft 2 5/8in (128.4cm), rear 4ft 2 5/16in (127. 8cm)
Overall width: 5ft 1in (155cm)
Overall height: 5ft 0in (152cm)
Overall length: 12ft 5in (379cm)
Overall weight, unladen kerb weight: 16½ cwt (839kg)

ELECTRICAL SYSTEM
Positive earth, 12 Volt, 43 AH battery mounted on tray in engine bay.
Lucas dynamo type C39PV/2 with compensated voltage control box and coil ignition.
Headlamps double dip 42/36 watt. Semaphore indicators 3 watt.

CAPACITIES
Fuel: 5 gallons (23.4 litres); engine oil: 6¾ pints (3.8 litres)

Hopes were high that the Travellers' car would prove popular in overseas markets. This left-hand drive model was photographed in Portugal.

COLOUR SCHEMES

October 1953 to October 1954

Paint colour	Trim colour	Floor covering
Birch Grey	Maroon	Black rubber mats
Black	Maroon	Black rubber mats
Clarendon Grey	Maroon	Black rubber mats
Empire Green	Green	Black rubber mats

October 1954 to September 1956

Paint colour	Trim colour	Floor covering
Black	Maroon	Maroon/Black *
Clarendon Grey	Maroon	Maroon/Black *
Empire Green	Green	Green/Black *
Sandy Beige **	Maroon	Maroon/Black *
Smoke Blue **	Maroon	Maroon/Black *

Notes:
*Black rubber mats were fitted to all Standard Travellers. However on De Luxe models maroon or green carpet was used to cover the front inner wheel arch panels.
** Smoke Blue was only used for a short period of time between October 1954 and February 1955 before being replaced by Sandy Beige.

CHAPTER 3
MINOR 1000 948cc TRAVELLER

MINOR 1000 948cc TRAVELLER

The Minor range was given a significant boost in the autumn of 1956 when a new model, the Morris Minor 1000, was announced at the London Motor Show. Development work had continued in order to restyle and revamp the Morris Minor, the main priority being to improve performance. To maintain its success and high levels of sale both at home and overseas, it was vital that any changes made should further enhance the Minor's already well-established reputation. Sid Goble oversaw the final stages of the development of the new car, and must have been delighted by the reaction to it at the show, and subsequently in the motoring press.

Externally, the most visible change was that the rather dated split windscreen, which in many ways was a throwback to pre World War Two days, had been replaced by a large one-piece curved windscreen between narrower pillars, thus improving forward visibility. By the nature of its design, the Traveller did not benefit from the other new styling features introduced on the saloon models, including improved rearward visibility thanks to a larger rear window and a changed roof profile. However, the Traveller did acquire the revised badges denoting Morris 1000, which were fixed on either side of the bonnet, and to the bottom of the right-hand rear door.

Internally, additions to the Morris 1000 Traveller, as it was now often known, mirrored those adopted on the rest of the range. Lids for the glove boxes on both sides of the fascia were new and so was a black-rimmed, dished three-spoke steering wheel, with a Morris motif in the centre. Changes were also made to the controls, with a combined indicator stalk and horn push fitted to the steering column. Changes to the interior trim were minimal on the early Morris 1000 Travellers. The seats were similar to those used on the Series II models. The only notable distinguishing feature was the use of contrast-colour piping on the seat edges.

The changes made to the mechanical specification were of greater significance. For those lamenting the shortcomings of the 803cc engine and wide-ratio gearbox, help was at hand. The new 948cc version of the A-series engine with output boosted to 37bhp at 4750 rpm was in itself a welcome improvement, but when mated to a much better gearbox with remote control change, the result was beyond expectations. Even for the slightly heavier Traveller model, acceleration was improved, and in-gear performance was significantly better than the Series II, with 36mph (58 km/h) obtainable in second, 59mph (95 km/h) in third and 70mph (113 km/h) in top.

From a driving point of view, the marked improvement in

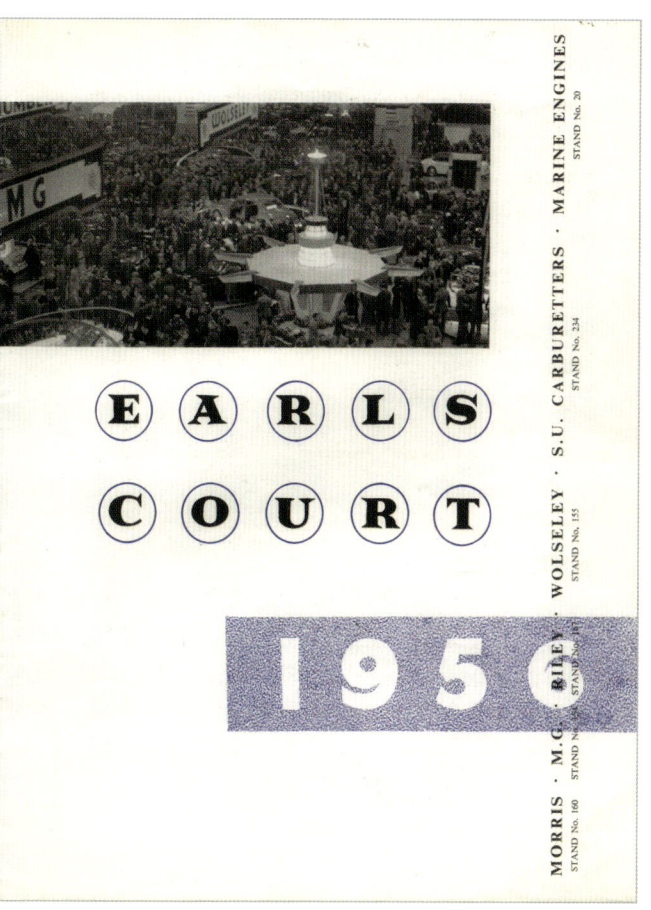

1956 was a key year in the development of the Morris Minor. The new Morris 1000 range, including the Traveller, was announced at the Earls Court Motor Show.

The Traveller model adopted the curved one-piece windscreen which gave a much more modern appearance.

The curved windscreen tells us that this is a Minor 1000, and the white sidelamps denote the 948cc version. Revised badges denoting Morris 1000 were fixed on either side of the bonnet and to the bottom of the right-hand rear door.

MORRIS MINOR TRAVELLER – THE COMPLETE COMPANION

The 948cc engine transformed the performance of the Morris 1000 range and was justifiably praised for smoothness and rugged reliability.

Extract from an early Morris 1000 sales brochure, showing key features of the new model. Note the interior trim with contrasting coloured piping on the seats.

the smoothness and operation of the gearbox, aided by the remote control gear change and better synchromesh, put the Minor 1000 at the top of its class. In most other respects, the Minor 1000 Traveller retained the previous specification, but could be clearly distinguished from the earlier split-screen models by the changes to front end styling.

ADVERTISING AND MARKETING

The introduction of the new up-rated model allowed the publicity department to adopt a fresh approach to promoting the Minor range. High on the list of priorities was emphasising the improved performance and the qualities of the '950cc' engine, as it was called in early brochures. The established 'in house' style was retained for the promotion of the Traveller, with marque slogans, such as 'Quality First' and 'Together You'll Choose a Morris' dominating the strap lines. The Traveller was described as the vehicle which 'Goes Anywhere – Does Anything' with the emphasis firmly on its versatility. Some interesting claims were made, including the fact that the Traveller, even with four people on board, offered more luggage space than that available in two ordinary saloons! Elsewhere information was included about the structure of the Traveller body. Described as strong but lightweight, it was said to be reinforced by the use of European ash, and with an eye to potential export markets, it was pointed out that the ash was protected sufficiently well for it to withstand tropical conditions. In fact the claims went further than that. According to the brochure 'All over the world – it's the Traveller everyone wants'.

Economy was highlighted in contemporary advertising, but so too was the Minor's handling, steering and braking.

Early style grey interior, with new three-spoke dished steering wheel with Morris motif in the centre.

Dark Green Morris 1000 Traveller with matching coloured wheels and front grille slats. Though originally sold as a Standard model, it has overriders fitted.

A revised moulded rubber floor covering was required to fit the new gear lever position. There was excellent access to the rear compartment, due to folding and tipping passenger seat.

Uncovered rear loading area and painted inner wheel arches are original features of this particular Traveller.

PRESS REACTION

Immediate press reaction to the Morris Minor 1000 was extremely positive both at home and abroad. 'Zestful and mature' was the 'In a nutshell' verdict of the Australian motoring magazine *Wheels*. The consensus of the *Wheels* team was that 'The pint size Morris negotiates traffic with impish ease, sits down on tight corners with unruffled nonchalance, obeys the driver's slightest whim at all times, and steers so crisply, that the unanimous verdict of three different *Wheels* testers is that it is almost as much fun to drive as its racy, two-seater MG stable mates!'

Closer to home, *The Autocar* carried out a road test of a 1958 Morris 1000 Traveller De Luxe. Many aspects of the Traveller were praised, and its attributes as a dual-purpose

The changed designation of the model was discreetly noted by the addition of a Morris 1000 badge on the rear door. Corresponding badges were fitted to each side of the bonnet

These three photos are of the actual Morris Minor Traveller Deluxe which The Autocar *tested in 1958. The results are reported in the text.*

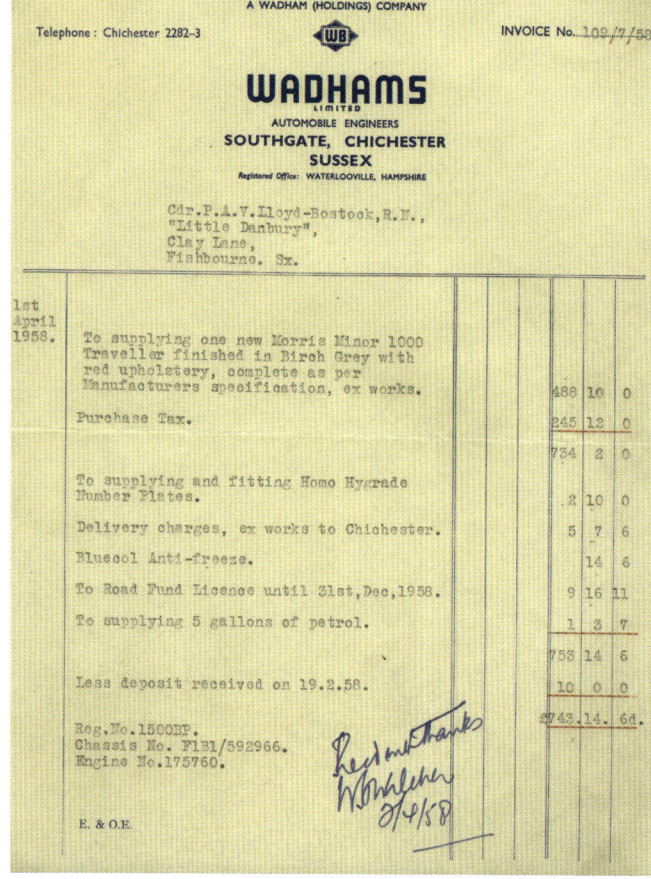

The Traveller models were generally the most expensive in the range. This sales invoice for a 1958 Morris Traveller totalled £753 14s 6d. Note the price of 5 gallons of petrol and the registration number!

vehicle were noted. Much was made of the new power unit, which was acknowledged to be smooth throughout the speed range, and to have a very responsive throttle reaction. The Traveller engine under test did not disappoint and the gearbox, rated as one of the best, was described as a pleasure to use. However, attention was drawn to both the increased weight of the Traveller model and its rectangular body shape, which combined to reduce the overall top speed by 4mph (6.4 km/h), when compared to a saloon model. On the other hand with a driver and one passenger, the Traveller could carry 360 lb (163kg), and even with four people on board (small people, weighing on average 9 stone or 57kg!) loading capacity was still 160 lb (73kg).

Other plus points included the steering which was described as high-geared, accurate, sensitive and light, and the all-round visibility courtesy of the rear side windows. The driver now even had a wing mirror as standard. Access to the rear compartment and the general build quality of the ash frame were items singled out for comment. For a small two-door car, access to the rear compartment with the passenger seat folded forward was deemed to be excellent, and the ease with which the sliding rear side windows could be operated, spoke volumes for the build quality of the wood frame.

Criticisms were confined to the comfort of the seats and the

NUFFIELD ORGANIZATION PRICE LIST

MORRIS	Home Retail Price £ s. d.	Purchase Tax £ s. d.	Total Price £ s. d.
Minor 1000 2-door Saloon	416 0 0	209 7 0	625 7 0
Minor 1000 2-door Saloon (De-luxe model)	433 10 0	218 2 0	651 12 0
Minor 1000 Convertible	416 0 0	209 7 0	625 7 0
Minor 1000 Convertible (De-luxe model)	433 10 0	218 2 0	651 12 0
Minor 1000 4-door Saloon	441 0 0	221 17 0	662 17 0
Minor 1000 4-door Saloon (De-luxe model)	462 0 0	232 7 0	694 7 0
Minor 1000 Traveller	471 10 0	237 2 0	708 12 0
Minor 1000 Traveller (De-luxe model)	488 10 0	245 12 0	734 2 0
Cowley 1500 Saloon	555 10 0	279 2 0	834 12 0
Oxford Saloon (Series III)	589 0 0	295 17 0	884 17 0
Oxford Traveller (Series IV)	665 0 0	333 17 0	998 17 0
Isis Saloon (Series II)	607 0 0	304 17 0	911 17 0
Isis Saloon (De-luxe model) (Series II)	640 0 0	321 7 0	961 7 0
Borg-Warner Overdrive (Isis only)	42 10 0	21 5 0	63 15 0
Manumatic Clutch (Oxford Saloon only)	33 6 8	16 13 4	50 0 0
Automatic Gearbox (Isis Saloon)	105 0 0	52 10 0	157 10 0
Extra for Duotone (Isis and Oxford Saloon, and Oxford Traveller Series IV)	10 0 0	5 0 0	15 0 0

M.G.			
Series MGA	663 0 0	332 17 0	995 17 0
Series MGA Coupé	724 0 0	363 7 0	1,087 7 0
M.G. Magnette Saloon (Single Colour)	714 0 0	358 7 0	1,072 7 0
M.G. Magnette Saloon (Varitone)	740 0 0	371 7 0	1,111 7 0
Manumatic Clutch (Magnette only)	33 6 8	16 13 4	50 0 0

HOME RETAIL EX-WORKS PRICES
These are the ex-Works prices obtaining at the date of publication and, with the specifications, they are liable to alteration from time to time without notice.

RILEY	Home Retail Price £ s. d.	Purchase Tax £ s. d.	Total Price £ s. d.
Two-Point-Six Saloon	940 0 0	471 7 0	1,411 7 0
Borg-Warner Overdrive	42 10 0	21 5 0	63 15 0
Automatic Gearbox	105 0 0	52 10 0	157 10 0
One-Point-Five Saloon (Heater and Windshield Washer standard)	575 0 0	288 17 0	863 17 0

WOLSELEY			
Fifteen Hundred Saloon	530 0 0	266 7 0	796 7 0
Fifteen-Fifty Saloon	660 0 0	331 7 0	991 7 0
Six-Ninety Saloon (Series III)	850 0 0	426 7 0	1,276 7 0
Borg-Warner Overdrive (Six-Ninety only)	42 10 0	21 5 0	63 15 0
Manumatic Clutch (Fifteen-Fifty Saloon only)	33 6 8	16 13 4	50 0 0
Automatic Gearbox (Six-Ninety Saloon only)	105 0 0	52 10 0	157 10 0
Duotone (Fifteen Hundred only)	10 0 0	5 0 0	15 0 0

PRINCESS			
Princess IV Saloon with Automatic Gearbox	2,250 0 0	1,126 7 0	3,376 7 0
Princess IV Touring Limousine, with Automatic Gearbox	2,360 0 0	1,181 7 0	3,541 7 0
Optional Extra (all models): Radio (Facia Controls)	35 0 0	17 10 0	52 10 0
Princess L.W.B. Saloon	2,150 0 0	1,076 7 0	3,226 7 0
Princess L.W.B. Limousine	2,150 0 0	1,076 7 0	3,226 7 0
Optional Extras (L.W.B.): Automatic Gearbox	193 10 0	96 15 0	290 5 0
Servo-assisted Brakes (L.W.B. only)	15 0 0	7 10 0	22 10 0
NOTE. When Automatic Transmission is supplied on L.W.B. models, Servo-assisted Brakes must be fitted.			
Radio (Rear Arm Rest Controls)	40 0 0	20 0 0	60 0 0

The exhaustive Nuffield price list from 1958 started off with all the different Minor 1000 models, eight in total, which made it the most prolific model range of the company.

adjustment for the driver's seat. The considered view was that 'the driving seat is rather primitive and does not allow the seat to be moved sufficiently far from the pedals for the comfort of a long-legged driver.' Criticism was also levelled at the driving position which was compromised by the seat squab being too high, and the steering wheel too big for such a small car. The newly installed indicator stalk, which had the horn push on the end, was condemned for causing inadvertent signalling, and not being self cancelling.

In spite of these niggling problems, the Traveller was roundly praised and though its design as a dual-purpose vehicle was accepted as a compromise, it still had plenty to offer: economy, ability to cover the ground rapidly if free use was made of the indirect gears, and handling qualities that were above average. For the price of £734 2s, including £245 12s Purchase Tax (now 60 per cent), £82 10s more than for a Morris Minor Saloon De Luxe, the Traveller owner not only enjoyed greater usefulness and convenience, but also a standard of body appointment and finish which was superior to that of most cars of comparable size.

The popular reception for the Morris Minor 1000 was not confined to the motoring press. Sustained sales provided the proof, if any were needed, that BMC had a winner on their hands. In the period from 1956 to 1962, adjustments to the specification concentrated mainly on changes to paint colours and interior trim, notably the introduction of the duo-tone interior trim on De Luxe models in 1961 (see below). There were general updates to improve instrumentation and lighting, and the inclusion of specific items in anticipation of future legislation. Mechanical updates were few, the most notable being the change from the large and imposing AC oil-bath air cleaner to the smaller more refined 'saucepan type' Cooper paper element type air cleaner in February 1959. The capacity of the fuel tank on Traveller models was increased in March 1957 from 5 gallons (23 litres) to 6½ gallons (30 litres).

LATER CHANGES

In the final years of 948cc Morris 1000 production, a number of small but significant changes were made. The Traveller roof lining was changed in 1957 when the rexine covered board headlining was replaced by a two piece headlining, similar in style and colour to the saloon headlining. In August 1961, a windscreen washer was included in the specification for De Luxe models, and seat belt anchorage points were built into all models. At the same time, the long-overdue decision was made to replace semaphore indicators on home market models with flashing indicators. It was a belated

Dating from March 1959 and finished in Frilford Grey paintwork, this Morris 1000 has undergone a complete restoration to a high standard.

move, given that from 1958, flashing indicators had been standard on export models, and prior to that could be specified as an optional extra. However, any hopes there may have been of having amber-coloured flashing lights were dashed, as the system relied on the fitting of a special relay which operated the front side lights and the rear brake lights, allowing them to flash. The wait for improved amber indicators extended beyond the end of 948cc Traveller production in September 1962.

A precise breakdown of the number of 948cc Travellers built is not available for the whole of the period from 1956 to 1962, though it is known that from 1959 onwards, some 63,820 were produced (including 1098cc models in 1962, see chapter 5). Those that survive are interesting vehicles in their own right, due to the variety of specifications which were available during the six-year production run. When on display they often prompt discussions amongst fellow enthusiasts. One of the most commonly asked questions from members of the public who see a Traveller with semaphore indicators is, 'Do they work?'

MINOR 1000 948cc TRAVELLER

Sensibly enough, the present-day owner has chosen not to rely on the sempahore indicators alone, and has fitted additiional amber flashers front and rear.

The registration mark 540 FRO tells us that this car was registered in Hertfordshire in March 1959.

As-new interior shows to good effect the features of the spacious load area of the Traveller model. The small pin and chain is an owner-added safety feature, to help secure the door stay locking mechanism.

MORRIS MINOR TRAVELLER – THE COMPLETE COMPANION

Glove box lids were part of the 948cc specification until they were discontinued in 1961. The remote gear lever was introduced with the 948cc engine.

Semaphore Indicators were eventually phased out on home market models in August 1961.

MINOR 1000 948CC TRAVELLER

Ongoing problems with the combined indicator switch and horn push were eventually solved in 1959 when the horn push returned to the centre of the steering wheel. The version shown here has the warning light for the indicators on the stalk, which has the horn push at the end of the lever.

Interior trim changes were frequent during the Morris 1000 948cc production run. This is the second type used. It features leather-faced seats with broad panels on both the seat back and squab. The seats shown are original.

41

This Minor 1000 has the later-type Cooper air cleaner that was introduced in 1959.

Contemporary press releases emphasised the business potential for the Traveller, as well as stressing its suitability for use as a private family vehicle.

MINOR 1000 948cc TRAVELLER SPECIFICATIONS 1956-62

ENGINE
Cast-iron block and head, pressed steel sump, four cylinders in line with pushrod-operated overhead valves
Bore and stroke: 62.9mm x 76.2mm; capacity: 948cc
Compression: 8:3:1 (high compression engine)
Maximum power: 37bhp at 4750rpm
Maximum torque: 50 lb/ft at 2500rpm
Fuel pump: SU type L
Carburettor: SU type H2 1¼in
Air cleaner: AC CL oil bath; Cooper dry type with paper element from February 1959

TRANSMISSION
Front engine, rear wheel drive. Four-speed gearbox in unit with engine. Synchromesh on second, third, and top gears. Remote control gear change.
Clutch: Borg and Beck single dry plate 6¼in (157mm).
Gear ratios: first 3.628:1; second; 2.374:1; third 1.412:1; top 1.000:1; reverse 4:664:1
Final drive: hypoid bevel three-quarter floating axle; ratio 4.55:1 or 9:41
Overall ratios: first 16.507:1, second 10.802:1, third 6.425:1, top 4.55:1; reverse 21.221:1

SUSPENSION
Front: independent by torsion bars and links, lever-arm hydraulic shock absorbers
Rear: half elliptic seven-leaf springs, lever-arm hydraulic shock absorbers

BRAKES
Lockheed hydraulic, 7in inch drums (178mm)
Front: two leading shoes; rear: one leading and one trailing shoe

STEERING
Rack and pinion, 2½ turns lock to lock; turning circle 33ft (10m)

WHEELS AND TYRES
Wheels: 14in pressed steel disc with four bolt fixing; tyres 5.00 x 14

DIMENSIONS AND WEIGHT
Wheelbase: 7ft 2in (218.4cm)
Track: front 4ft 2 5/8 in (128.4cm), rear 4ft 2 5/16 in (127.8cm)
Overall width: 5ft 1in (155cm)
Overall height: 5ft 0in (152cm)
Overall length: 12ft 5in (379cm)
Overall weight, with 5 gallons of fuel: 16¼cwt (1827 lbs or 829kg)

ELECTRICAL SYSTEM
Positive earth, 12 Volt, 43 AH battery mounted on tray in engine bay. Lucas dynamo type C39PV/2 with compensated voltage control box and coil ignition. Headlamps double dip 42/36 watt. Semaphore indicators 3 watt.

CAPACITIES
Fuel: 5 gallons (23 litres), from March 1957 6½ gallons (30 litres); engine oil: 7 pints (4 litres)

COLOUR SCHEMES

The 948c Travellers were not finished in the full range of colours available for the rest of the Minor range at the same time.

October 1956 to February 1959

Paint	Trim	Carpet *
Birch Grey	Red	Maroon
Black	Red	Maroon
Black	Green	Beagle Green
Clarendon Grey	Red	Maroon
Dark Green	Grey	Black

February 1959 to July 1960

Paint	Trim	Carpet *
Black	Red	Red
Clipper Blue	Blue-Grey	Blue
Frilford Grey	Red	Red
Sage Green	Green	Beagle Green

July 1960 to October 1961

Paint	Trim	Carpet *
Black	Red	Red
Old English White	Red	Red
Smoke Grey	Blue-Grey	Blue
Yukon Grey	Red	Red

October 1961 to October 1962

Paint	Trim **	Carpet *
Almond Green	Porcelain Green, with Silver Beige	Almond Green
Black	Tartan Red, with Silver Beige	Tartan Red
Old English White	Tartan Red, with Silver Beige	Tartan Red
Rose Taupe	Tartan Red, with Silver Beige	Tartan Red
Smoke Grey	Blue-Grey, with Silver Beige	Blue

A fine resting place for this 1960 Clipper Blue Morris 1000 Traveller.

Notes: * The carpet colours are for De Luxe models. Standard models were fitted with black moulded rubber mats. ** De Luxe models had duo-tone trim partly in Silver Beige.

Three main interior trim styles were used on the 948cc Travellers between 1956 and 1962. These can be summarised as follows:
(1) Fluted pattern seats with plain matching door cards and rear side panels. This trim style was used between 1956 and 1959, and usually had contrast-colour piping.
(2) Broad patterned seats with plain matching door cards and rear side panels. This second type was used from early 1959 until 1961. On Travellers, it was available in three colours, Blue-Grey, Green, and Red (on saloons and tourers, Oxford Beige could also be found). De Luxe models had leather seat facings.
(3) From October 1961, De Luxe models were fitted with duo-tone patterned seats with matching duo-tone door cards, but plain monotone rear side panels. The seats and door trim panels had Silver Beige inserts which contrasted with either Blue-Grey, Porcelain Green, or Tartan Red vynide. Standard models had similarly-patterned monotone colour seats with monotone door cards and side panels. The duo-tone style was carried forward on the 1098cc model, introduced in 1962. The introduction of the duo-tone vynide trim brought to an end the practice of using leather seat facings on De Luxe Travellers.

Floor and rear load area coverings

A revised rubber front floor covering was introduced for the 948cc Travellers, to allow for the changed gear lever position. De Luxe Travellers were fitted with carpets matching the main interior trim colour. The use of a two-piece floor covering in durable grey Hardura for the rear load compartment which was also attached to the back of the rear seat squab continued on De Luxe models. It provided much-needed protection to the load area and was held in place by aluminium strips. During the course of 948 cc production, the use of this material was extended to provide a covering for the inner wheel arches for all models

Wheel and radiator grille colours

During 948cc production the colour used on wheels and grilles changed. From 1956 the pattern adopted was that with the exception of Travellers finished in Dark Green or Black, the wheels and grille would be painted body colour. In the case of Black cars, both the wheels and the grille bars were painted Birch Grey. Dark Green cars had Birch Grey wheels and body-coloured grille bars. From February 1959, almost all Travellers had contrast-colour wheels and grille bars. Pearl Grey was used until July 1960, after which Old English White was adopted. Any Travellers finished in Old English White had matching wheels and grille bars.

MORRIS MINOR TRAVELLER – THE COMPLETE COMPANION

CHAPTER 4
MINOR 1000 1098CC TRAVELLER

MINOR 1000 1098cc TRAVELLER

By the autumn of 1962, expectations were high that the anticipated upgrade being planned for the Morris Minor range would be an extensive one. In the event, there was a feeling of disappointment, as the changes made were limited to the major mechanical components. It was reminiscent of the situation which occurred when the Series II mechanical changes were made in 1953. In keeping with the rest of the range, the Traveller received the new larger capacity 1098cc engine, first introduced in August 1962 on the Morris 1100, a changed gearbox, and improved brakes.

Preliminary work had begun in February 1962 when a Minor saloon was fitted with the larger engine. Extensive testing occurred before the go-ahead was given for the Minor to be included as part of a rationalisation programme which saw the 1098cc engine being introduced across the BMC range. The Austin A40 and the A35 van, the MG Midget and the Austin-Healey Sprite, all benefitted from the increased power offered by the new engine. In the Minor, performance was markedly improved, thanks to a higher compression ratio of 8.5.1 and 48bhp at 5100rpm. The engine was a robust unit which had a strengthened crankcase and stronger internal components, particularly the crankshaft. It was mated to a much-improved gearbox which had a ribbed casing to provide extra strength. Baulk-ring synchromesh and a larger clutch were welcome additions, which gave a more positive and lighter feel to the gear change. A higher rear axle ratio offered more relaxed cruising and improved in-gear performance, albeit with a fairly modest top speed of 74mph (119 km/h).

With the extra power and performance that was now available, it was important to incorporate some improvements to the braking system. Drum brakes were retained, but in an effort to improve stopping power, 8in (203mm) drums were introduced for the front brakes. No change was deemed necessary for the rear where the use of 7in (178mm) drums continued. The upgrades did not extend to the suspension. In

The 1962 Traveller brochure heralded the introduction of the 1098cc overhead valve engine and continued Morris's Quality First theme.

The 1098cc models were destined to be the last of the Morris Minor Travellers. They remained in production for almost a decade.

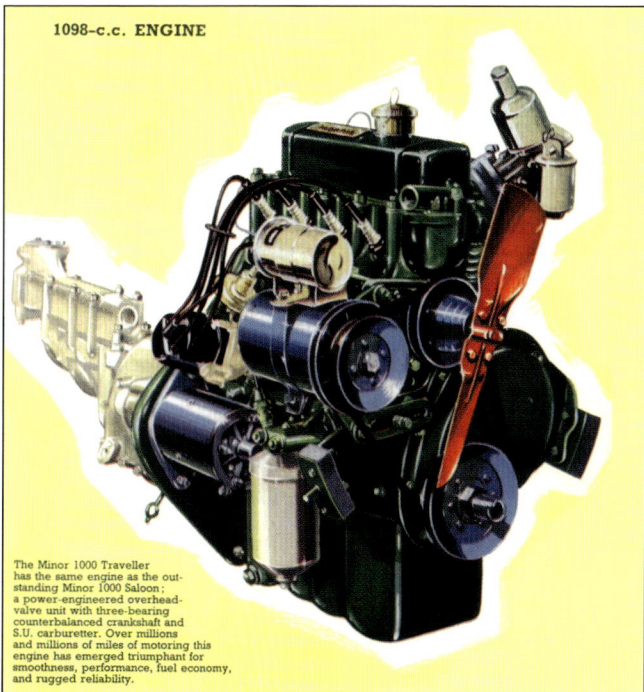

The credentials of the new 1098cc engine were highlighted to good effect.

spite of the tendency for axle tramp to manifest itself when cornering in 'power down' mode, no remedial action was deemed necessary. Even with the increased power available, it was felt that the highly regarded suspension design, which had remained unchanged since 1948, would still suffice.

The Minors, including the Traveller, which were built between October 1962 and September 1964, have become known as 'interim' or 'transitional' models, mainly because they effectively bridged the gap between the 948cc models and the final major revamp of the model range, which took place a full two years after the 1098cc engine was introduced. The 'in-betweeners' as they have become known, have some interesting features. The interior trim style introduced for the last of the 948cc cars was carried forward, with duo-tone upholstery on De Luxe models and single-colour upholstery, using a similar pattern, on standard models. The glove boxes were once again open cubby holes on both sides.

Other features carried over from the 948cc models included the three-spoke steering wheel, bronze-faced speedometer, light-coloured crash pad covering, and small solid sun visors, as well as the 'clap hands' windscreen wipers. Further examples of continuity included some of the engine ancillaries, such as the screw-type fittings on the fuse and control boxes, and the screw-type connector for the high-tension lead on the coil. From August 1961, the front side lights and rear tail lamps had been used as indicators on all models, but a major update of the lighting arrangement occurred in October 1963. At the front, large circular side lamps with a part-amber lens for indicators were positioned beneath the headlamps. This much-improved arrangement was adopted across the whole range including the Traveller.

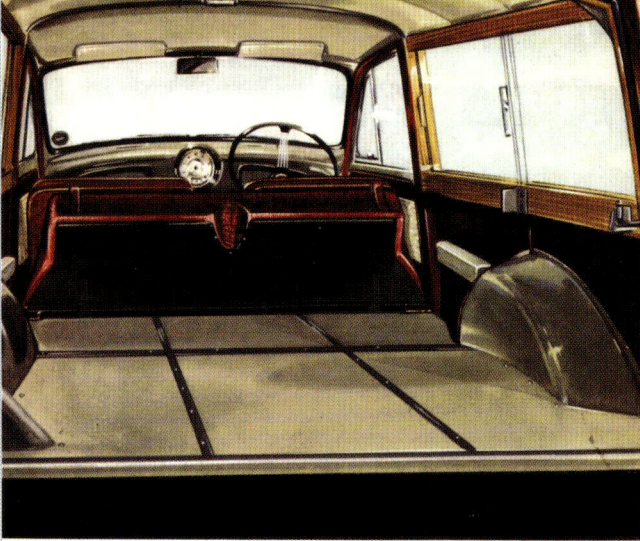

Press photographs followed the same theme, principally because the 1962 update concentrated on a major mechanical update.

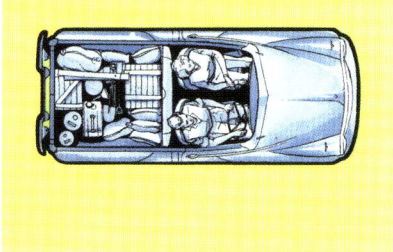

In two quick movements the rear seat folds flat, giving ample room for carrying anything from full camping equipment to loads of merchandise of every shape and kind. Never before has such space been achieved within such modest external dimensions.

Sleeves rolled up...or ready for fun

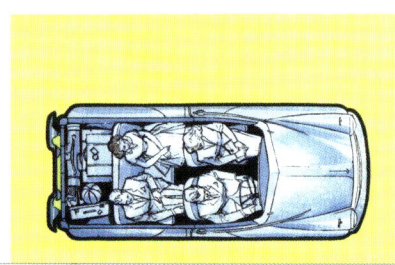

Driver, three passengers, and as much luggage as you could carry in the trunks of two ordinary saloons! The strong but lightweight body is reinforced with selected European ash, preserved to withstand tropical conditions.

MINOR 1000 1098cc TRAVELLER

This little Traveller goes to market—with a much wider profit margin for the grower who knows his onions.

Green, green pastures . . . The Traveller carries you there and back with maximum economy and the minimum of fuss.

Down to the sea in ships—and now you can combine the thrills of sea-fever with the pleasures of 'space' travel!

Tom Brown's school-days are twice as much fun—and a service to friends is no trouble at all as there is lots of room to spare.

Wheels within wheels—and Junior's birthday present comes home without a scratch, thanks to all that space in the back!

When Mr. Jones builds his dream house the Traveller keeps his costs down and his bank manager happy.

Family reunion—and the old folks marvel as the young 'uns show how it's done. They never thought it would all go in.

Even a what-not's not a problem when treasured possessions have to find a new home; the Traveller gets quietly on with the job.

The virtues of the Traveller were presented in a variety of ways including cartoons and inventive line drawings.

47

MORRIS MINOR TRAVELLER – THE COMPLETE COMPANION

This 1963 Morris Traveller has the updated combined front indicator and side light arrangement introduced in October 1963.

However at the rear, the Traveller models had to make do with just additional separate round indicators with slightly larger domed amber lenses, while saloon and tourer models benefitted from a much more prominent new style combined indicator, stop and tail light cluster, mounted in an attractive chrome bezel. Around the same time, the 'clap hands' wipers were replaced by parallel-working wipers, and the front passenger (left-hand) door gained an external key lock.

The use of plain coloured interior rear side panels was a feature of the Traveller specification.

The interior still exhibits many of the features common to the 948cc model interior specifications; note for example the steering wheel, speedometer and sun visors.

MINOR 1000 1098CC TRAVELLER

The open glove boxes on both sides were a feature of early 1098cc models.

The Silver Beige contrast colour was found on the wheelarches and elbow rests in the rear compartment.

The essential features of the duotone interior are illustrated here. The passenger seat folded and tipped forward to allow easy access to the rear compartment.

MORRIS MINOR TRAVELLER – THE COMPLETE COMPANION

This fine example of a late model Traveller finished in striking Maroon 'B' paintwork still retains the essential character of the original design.

THE LAST MAJOR UPDATE IN 1964

The long awaited major revamp of the Minor range eventually took place in October 1964. It concentrated mainly on updating the interior specification, improving some aspects of safety, and enhancing comfort levels. Elsewhere in the BMC range, most notably on the new 1100 models, the use of heat-formed vinyl seat and trim panels had proved successful. Its use in the Morris Minor, using a carefully selected range of colours enhanced by matching carpet and door seals, produced a light and airy feel to the interior. In the case of the Traveller, front and rear seats and the front door cards incorporated the distinctive fluted panels but, unlike saloons and tourers, all the rear side panels remained plain.

A simple but effective rear lighting arrangement with an understated Morris 1000 badge on the rear door gave the rear of the vehicle an uncluttered look.

MINOR 1000 1098cc TRAVELLER

The black-faced speedometer, revised switch controls and the colour-coded glove box lid, which were all features of the revised fascia on the post-1964 vehicles, were well received, as was the two spoke steering wheel and the heat formed vinyl trim used on the seats and door panels.

The fascia was also changed. A new-look speedometer with an imposing black face was mounted in an anodized panel, flanked by two vertical chrome strips. There were new switches for the main controls, and a key-operated combined ignition lock and starter switch. A glove box lid was added on the passenger side, while the driver still had an open compartment. Concessions to safety included a change to the dished steering wheel which now had two spokes, with a centrally-placed horn push. A plastic framed interior mirror, together with crushable sun visors which swivelled so that they could be positioned next to the side windows, plus a black vinyl-covered crash pad on the leading edge of the parcel shelf were additional safety features.

A much more efficient 2.8kw heater with a fresh-air facility improved ventilation considerably, and allowed for quicker demisting and heat circulation. An even bigger 3.8kw version was available as an optional extra. A new push-pull heater control situated inside the car, which allowed for adjustment to the water valve mounted on top of the engine, was another welcome change. Previously, adjustment had to be carried out by turning a tap in the engine bay.

In subsequent years, there were some slight adjustments to certain components. For example, the bonnet motif which had been of composite construction became a one-piece mazak casting with the M motif painted red, and the windscreen rubber insert changed from a two-piece metal fixing with a covering joining piece, to a one-piece chrome-effect plastic extrusion with no additional fixing. Provision had been made for fitting front seat belts in 1961, and from June 1964 onwards, it was common practice for dealers to fit static seat belts as standard, and inertia reel belts as an optional extra. However, it was not until very late in Traveller production, from 1 January 1971, that it became mandatory to fit front seat belts as part of the standard factory specification.

The expansive loading area, which remained unchanged as far as overall capacity was concerned, was improved by the addition of hard-wearing material and aluminium rubbing strips in the load area

PRESS REACTION

Reaction to the 1964 update was fairly positive within the dealer network, as it was felt that the changes provided new impetus for home market sales. Regrettably overseas sales were on the decline, due mainly to competition from other, newer BMC cars, including the Mini and 1100. Both of these models were also offered in Traveller versions which undoubtedly had an impact on potential Morris 1000 Traveller sales. Denmark at least remained a good market, and the Danes called the 1098cc version the Morris 1000 Super (see also chapter 6).

In the UK, *Motor* chose to road test a De Luxe Traveller in 1965. In a comprehensive analysis undertaken twelve years after the Traveller entered production, there was an understandable desire to establish whether the still-popular Traveller was keeping pace with modern developments. The results were mixed, even though the overall assessment was that the Traveller carried its age well, was reasonably comfortable for four passengers, able to carry quite large and heavy loads, and was a good dual-purpose vehicle which represented value for money, at £606 18s9d including Purchase Tax.

On the positive side, the body styling of the Traveller or estate car as it was now referred to, was deemed not to be old-fashioned; indeed it was kindly said that 'When a car has been in production as long as the Minor, age can be a virtue which gives time for all the little design faults to be ironed out.' The performance of the 1098cc engine was praised. In a comparison with six competitors, the Morris Minor Traveller out-performed contemporaries such as the Ford Anglia estate, the Hillman Husky, the Austin A40 Countryman, the Mini Countryman, and the Renault 4L in terms of acceleration. From 0-50mph (0-80 km/h) it was beaten only by the Fiat 1100D estate. However, it failed to outperform many of these vehicles in terms of maximum speed, a fact that the road tester choose to attribute to 'the bulbous and evidently unaerodynamic design which clearly takes its toll causing acceleration to fall off sharply.' The Minor reached an average of 73.2mph (117.8 km/h) while the Fiat was fastest at just over 83mph (133.5 km/h).

Concerns were also expressed about the noise levels inside the car. These too were attributed to the design of the Traveller, with specific reference being made to first and second gears, the rear axle, and the fact that the relatively empty van-like interiors of estate cars such as the Traveller 'sometimes form ideal resonant cavities.' In a rather telling comment, which says as much about the road tester, as the car, he laments the fact that when travelling on the motorway, 'the radio has to be turned up to distortion level if the piano passages are to be heard'!

Seating, though described as reasonably comfortable, was criticised for lack of adjustment on the driver's side. In fact, it was rather bluntly described as inadequate. Further negative comment was made about the ride, which was described as somewhat stiff and bouncy. With seat belts fitted, it was felt that the driver and front passenger were forced into 'unpleasant vertical oscillations between the seat and the seat belt when driving over rough surfaces.'

Other constructive criticisms related to the rather minimal tool kit which was supplied in a 'cheap, wrinkled plastic holdall', and to the operation of the jack. In a legitimate gripe the point was forcefully made that unless the door was opened before jacking up the car, the wheel brace which also served as a crank for turning the screw type jack could not be turned for a full revolution, without brushing against the car and marking the paintwork.

In this particular road test, the Traveller was thoroughly appraised, even allowing for the fact that the road tester had a particularly bad day, as a cloudburst caused water to leak through the windscreen rubber, and obscured the view through the rear windows. There was much to suggest that the Morris 1000 Traveller still had a lot to offer the discerning motorist who required an attractive, economical, dual-purpose vehicle with 30 cu.ft (810 litres) of useable load space and a carrying capacity of 5cwt (254kg) with the driver only, or four adults and 100 lbs (45kg).

A minimal tool kit, comprising a jack, combined wheel brace and starting handle, a tommy bar and a wheel disc remover was issued a standard on 1098cc Travellers. An option to purchase a more comprehensive tool kit was offered.

EXPERIMENTAL WOOD EFFECT FRAMES

In the later years of production, consideration was given to reducing the overall costs of producing the Morris 1000 Traveller. Attention focussed on the wood frame bodywork, which was expensive and complicated to make by 1960s standards (see also chapter 5). Alternative sources were explored for the supply of the ash for the wood frame, and timber was imported from as far afield as Poland in an effort to reduce margins. Various other ideas were explored, including the replacement of the solid wood rear pillars with laminated wood pillars. These were put into production but proved to be of inferior quality, due mainly to the fact that they were vulnerable to the ingress of water and were prone to discolouration. They were eventually replaced with the original solid, one-piece version on later production models.

Without doubt the most radical attempt to replace the ash frame with an a more durable alternative was the experiment which involved making an aluminium frame covered with a wood effect GRP (glass fibre) moulding for use on the Minor Traveller. For many years after production ceased, there was much speculation about the viability of such an experiment, and many questioned the rumours that some vehicles actually left the factory with this type of frame fitted.

Confirmation that a limited number of Travellers, estimated to be fewer than ten, were released from the factory has emerged in recent years. Jim Collins, who worked in the Research and Development Department at the Cowley plant in Oxford, was involved in the design and construction of the experimental frame which was fitted to the Traveller. In what can only be described as a fortuitous turn of events, he decided to have his own recently-purchased Traveller photographed alongside one of the experimental vehicles at the factory in 1970. Fortunately the photographs remained in his possession, and when Jim eventually sold his Traveller, the photographs which provide authenticity to the story, passed to the current owner Leo Greenaway.

Further confirmation that at least one of the Travellers fitted with the GRP frame was released from the factory and offered for sale, emerged when a late-registered Traveller was photographed in Oxford in 1987. On close inspection, the

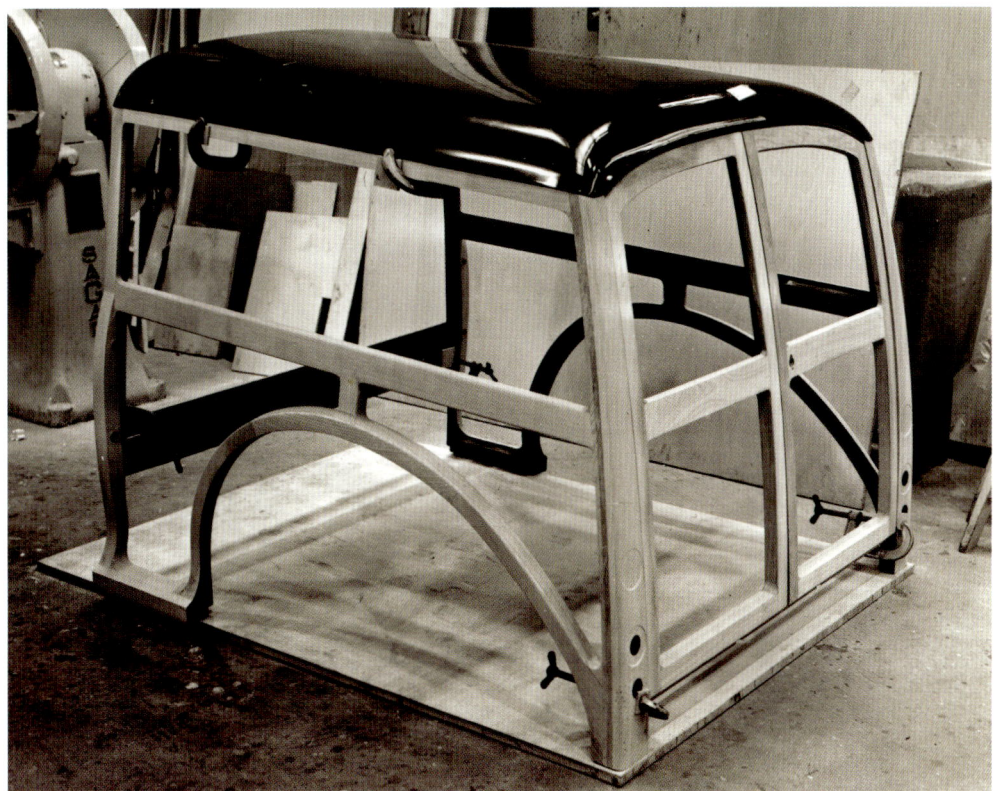

The wood effect glass fibre frame as developed in the Research and Development department at Cowley.

Spot the difference! These views show the standard Traveller (left) and the prototype with a glass fibre frame (right). Could this unregistered car be SFC 427J?

Close examination of the frame on this Traveller reveals the curved corners of the glass fibre version.

Registered SFC 427J, this glass fibre framed Traveller was photographed in Oxford in 1987 and is thought to be one of two survivors of the experiment to change the traditional ash frame.

GRP moulding which extended to the rear door frames was found to be in remarkably good condition, with no visible signs of cracking or splitting. It will remain a mystery whether it was on the grounds of economics, or the fact that the phasing-out of the Morris Minor had already begun and that the Traveller's days were therefore numbered, that the project did not proceed. Nevertheless, the feasibility of producing an alternative to the ash frame, while retaining the essential character of the Traveller had been proven, even if it was destined to be a short-lived experiment.

THE LATE TRAVELLERS

Traveller production moved to Adderley Park in Birmingham in 1969, following the creation of British Leyland Motor Corporation (BLMC), but the only changes were to the range of colour schemes. Some very striking colours were adopted for the late model Travellers, thanks in part to the extensive paint and trim colours used on other British Leyland vehicles.

Though sales held up well, little thought was given to developing or upgrading the Traveller models. In a concession to security, a steering column lock was introduced during the final months of production. This necessitated a slight change to the fascia panel, with a blanking plate being added where the ignition lock used to be. A further improvement was the introduction of an alternator to some of the last models to leave the production lines; it had already been fitted to some earlier Police vehicles (see chapter 7).

The end for the Traveller came in April 1971, when, without much fanfare or fuss, the assembly lines at Adderley Park fell silent. The demise of the Traveller did not quite mark the end of Morris Minor production in Britain, as the

Some late model Travellers were fitted with steering column locks. This additional safety measure was also used on late model vans and pick-ups.

As a result of fitting the steering column lock, a chrome disc was added to the fascia to cover the aperture for the key start ignition previously used.

MINOR 1000 1098cc TRAVELLER

This British Leyland brochure dating from 1970 which sought to promote the Traveller is the last brochure for the Morris Minor range as it was then. Interestingly it carried an addendum to say that reclining seats were no longer available on Traveller models, and that the basic Traveller was no longer available. It also stated that a steering lock was fitted as standard on home market models.

van and pick-up continued until December 1971. Saloon production at Cowley had ended in November 1970, but the last few batches of saloon CKD kits had been despatched from Cowley only in early 1971, and might still have remained to be assembled abroad for a little longer. While in one sense it marked the end of an era during which the Minor had established itself as a firm favourite both in Britain and overseas, it also marked the beginning of the post-production era, during which the Minor Traveller would continue to prove its worth by continuing to provide sound dependable transport, by demonstrating its capacity for further improvement and its potential for regeneration – as will be discussed later in this book.

A Lucas 11 AC alternator was fitted to some of the very last Travellers built at Adderley Park. Such engines had a special engine number prefix 10V-190-E-H.

Opposition to the well established Morris Minor Traveller in the form of the Morris 1300 Traveller probably influenced the decision to cease production in April 1971.

55

Note the warning stencilled on the top of the radiator fan shroud on this late-model Minor. 'Health and Safety' already!

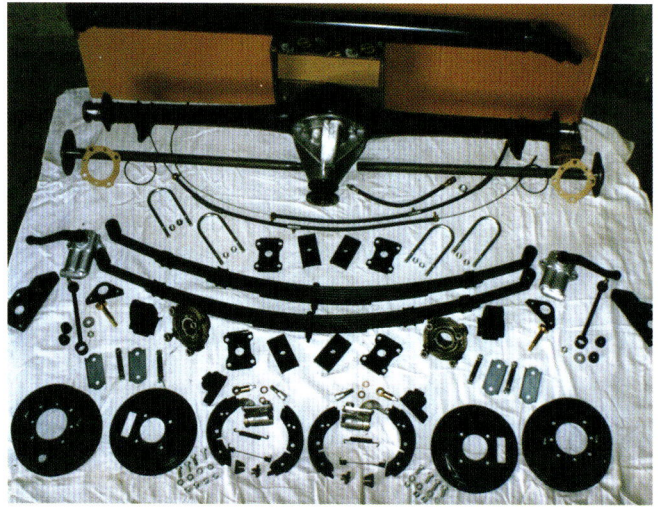

All the components required for a complete overhaul of the rear suspension, brakes etc. Note seven leaf springs as used on the Traveller models.

MINOR 1000 1098cc TRAVELLER SPECIFICATION 1962-71

ENGINE
Cast-iron block and head, pressed steel sump,
four cylinders in line with pushrod-operated overhead valves
Bore and stroke: 64.58mm x 83.72mm; capacity 1098cc
Compression ratio: 8:5:1 (high compression engine)
Maximum power: 48bhp at 5100rpm
Maximum torque: 60 lb/ft at 2500rpm
Fuel pump: SU type L
Carburettor: SU type HS2 1¼in
Air cleaner: Cooper dry type with paper element

TRANSMISSION
Front engine, rear wheel drive. Four-speed gearbox in unit with engine.
Synchromesh on second, third, and top gears. Remote control gear change.
Clutch: Borg and Beck single dry plate 7¼in (158.7mm)
Gear ratios: first 3:628:1; second; 2:172:1; third 1:412:1; top 1.000:1; reverse 4:664:1
Final drive: hypoid bevel three-quarter floating axle; ratio 4.220:1 or 9:38
Overall ratios: first 15.276:1, second 9.169:1, third 5.950:1, top 4.220:1; reverse 19.665:1

SUSPENSION
Front: independent by torsion bars and links, lever-arm hydraulic shock absorbers
Rear: half elliptic seven-leaf springs, lever-arm hydraulic shock absorbers

BRAKES
Lockheed hydraulic, 8in drums front (203mm), 7in drums rear (178mm)
Front: two leading shoes; rear one leading and one trailing shoe

STEERING
Rack and pinion, 2½ turns lock to lock, turning circle 33ft (10m)

WHEELS AND TYRES
Wheels: 14in pressed steel disc with four-bolt fixing; tyres 5.00 x 14

DIMENSIONS AND WEIGHT
Wheelbase: 7ft 2in (218.4cm)
Track: front 4ft 2 5/8 in (128.4cm), rear 4ft 2 5/16 in (127. 8cm)
Overall width: 5ft 1in (155cm)
Overall height: 5ft 0in (152cm)
Overall length: 12ft 5in (379cm)
Overall weight: 16½cwt (839kg); *Motor* 14 August 1965 quoted 15¾cwt (801kg)

ELECTRICAL SYSTEM
Positive earth, 12 Volt, 43 AH battery mounted on tray in engine bay.
Lucas dynamo type C40-1 with RB 106/2 control box and ignition coil LA 12
(some late cars were fitted with an alternator).
Flashing indicator unit FL5. Headlamps double dip 42/36 watt.

CAPACITIES
Fuel: 6½ gallons (30 litres); engine oil: 6½ pints (3.7 litres)

COLOUR SCHEMES

1962 to 1964

Paint	Trim *	Carpet **
Almond Green	Porcelain Green, with Silver Beige	Green
Black	Tartan Red, with Silver Beige	Red
Old English White	Tartan Red, with Silver Beige	Red
Rose Taupe	Tartan Red, with Silver Beige	Red
Smoke Grey	Blue-Grey, with Silver Beige	Blue

Notes: * De Luxe models had duo-tone trim partly in Silver Beige.
** The carpet colours are for De Luxe models. Standard models were fitted with black moulded rubber mats, until they were discontinued in early 1970.

1964 to 1967

Paint	Trim	Carpet
Almond Green	Porcelain Green	Green
Black	Cherokee Red	Red
Old English White	Cherokee Red	Red
Rose Taupe	Cherokee Red	Red
Smoke Grey	Blue-Grey	Blue

1967 to 1969

Paint	Trim	Carpet
Almond Green	Porcelain Green	Green
Black	Cherokee Red	Red
Maroon 'B'	Cherokee Red	Red
Peat Brown	Cherokee Red	Red
Smoke Grey	Blue-Grey	Blue
Snowberry White	Black	Black
Trafalgar Blue	Blue-Grey	Blue

1969 to 1970

Paint	Trim	Carpet
Bermuda Blue	Black	Black
Blue Royale	Galleon Blue	Blue
Connaught Green	Autumn Leaf	Brown
Cumulus Grey	Galleon Blue	Blue
Faun Brown	Autumn Leaf	Brown
White or Glacier White	Black	Black
White	Blue-Grey	Blue
White	Cherokee Red	Red
White	Porcelain Green	Green

June 1970 to April 1971

Paint	Trim	Carpet
Aqua	Navy Blue	Navy Blue
Bedouin	Autumn Leaf	Autumn Leaf
Bermuda Blue	Navy Blue	Navy Blue
Glacier White	Geranium	Red
Glacier White	Navy Blue	Navy Blue
Glacier White	Red	Red
Limeflower	Navy Blue	Navy Blue
Teal Blue	Limeflower	Olive

In the later years of production, particularly when production moved from Cowley to Adderley Park, the range of colour schemes increased dramatically.

A wide range of colours were offered on the late model Travellers including Limeflower which had navy interior trim.

CHAPTER 5
BUILDING THE TRAVELLER

Most of the work relating to preparation and assembly of the wood frame for both the Morris Oxford Series MO Traveller and the Minor Traveller took place in Coventry. The Morris Bodies Plant was spread out over two adjacent sites in the Quinton Road, Mile Lane, and Park Side area near to the centre of Coventry. It was here that thousands of Traveller wood frames were created from bare planks of ash which were sourced from different locations including Eastern Europe, and were transported to the saw mills by road.

The process of creating all the different components which made up the wood frame was both time consuming and labour intensive. Working conditions were often far from ideal and many workers suffered in later life from respiratory problems, due to the inhalation of dust. Many different types of saws and other items of woodworking equipment were used to transform the bare ash logs into the specially-shaped component parts of the Traveller frame.

Once delivered to the saw mills, the wood was cut into manageable lengths, using a crosscut saw. The sides of the rough lengths of wood were then tidied up, using a line saw and planer. Templates were used to mark out some of the more complex shapes, such as the curved pieces which made up the wood wheel arch section. These were then cut out using a band saw, and shaped using a special machine called a spindle. The pieces were held in position by special jigs while final shaping occurred.

Routers and tenoners were used to cut slots in the uprights, and to shape the tenons on the side rails. Obtaining the perfect finish required a substantial amount of sanding. Different methods were used for different components. Curved sections, such as the footer and the wheel arch pieces, were hand-held against the belt of a power sander, while

The Morris Bodies Plant at Coventry was responsible for the making and assembly of all the component parts of the ash frame. Depending on the requirements of different assembly plants, the rear sections were painted and for a time married to the front cab section, before onward despatch by road or rail. Attaching the assembled rear frame to the front cab section was a labour-intensive process, requiring skill and a good deal of patience.

BUILDING THE TRAVELLER

At Coventry, an air of traditional carriagework remained with the assembly of ash-framed Morris Traveller bodies.

Special arrangements were made at the Cowley plant to integrate the assembly of the Traveller on the main assembly lines. Here final checks are being made to lighting and wheel alignment.

straight parts, such as the cant rails and the waist rails, were put through a drum sander.

Once a satisfactory finish had been obtained, each individual part of the frame was placed in a hot Cuprinol dip for up to two hours, after which they were removed and placed on drying racks. Once dried, these parts were then transported to G block where the frames were assembled. At this stage, the rear doors were fitted and aligned. The aluminium panels were pre-cut, drilled, and painted, before being fixed to the varnished frames. The bodies were then prepared for transportation, usually by road, to the main assembly plant at Cowley. In the early years of production, quantities of the individual components were despatched, unassembled, to the CKD department ready for packing and transportation to overseas assembly plants.

PRODUCTION LINE ASSEMBLY

The introduction of the Traveller models prompted a major rethink of the assembly processes at the Cowley works in 1952. Given that substantial parts of the vehicle were being assembled in two different plants in Birmingham and Coventry some twenty miles apart, and then had to be transported south to Cowley, different strategies were needed to manage the eventual marriage of the cab and floor section with the rear body. In order to allow this to happen, a new sub-assembly area was created at Cowley. This was called the Body Loft. In this area, the already painted Traveller cab was joined together with the wood-frame rear body from the Coventry Bodies plant. In what could be, and apparently often was, a challenging operation, the body was aligned with the cab, and then joined with a series of bolts through the B-post and across the rear of the cab roof. Inserting and trimming the T-shaped rubber strip between the metal cab roof and the aluminium rear roof section was by all accounts a delicate operation, made more difficult by the need to ensure even tensioning, so that no rippling occurred in the weaker alloy material.

With the rest of the frame successfully aligned and secured, the whole Traveller shell could then proceed to the final assembly line. In the case of the Minor Traveller, this was Line Number 1. From the Body Loft, the Traveller shells were lowered on to the feeder track which in turn joined the main assembly line. This operation had to be carefully sequenced as the feeder track, which carried sixty assorted models an hour to the main assembly line, had to be managed so that the Travellers could be slotted in without adversely affecting the speed of the track. Once on the track the Travellers proceeded to final build with various sub assemblies common to the Minor range being added, as well as the model-specific components such as interior trim, headlining, rear bumper assembly, and lights.

THREE DIFFERENT ASSEMBLY PLANTS

Cowley was not the only assembly plant in the UK where the Minor Travellers were built. In 1960, due to a collapse of the sizeable American market for sports cars, the MG factory at Abingdon was faced with short-time working. Production of Minor light commercial and some Traveller models was switched from Cowley to Abingdon, initially for a six-month period. Four years later, Morris Minor assembly came to an end at the plant, by which time over 20,000 Morris Minor vans, pick-ups, and Travellers had been produced. Of this

59

total, over 50 per cent were Travellers. Meanwhile, the bulk of Travellers continued to be assembled at Cowley.

Assembly methods were similar to those at Cowley, the main exception being that complete Traveller bodies arrived at Abingdon already painted and ready for final assembly. This required a change to normal operations, with the cab and floor being transported to the Coventry Morris Bodies Plant from the Birmingham-based Nuffield Metal Products factory where the front end panels were pressed and assembled. In an expanded operation, these bodies were then painted at the Coventry plant, prior to the wood frame, complete with painted aluminium sides and roof, being added. Onward despatch to the assembly lines in the Abingdon plant for final build was undertaken by both road and rail.

Traveller production was concentrated at Cowley again in 1964, and remained there until the gradual phasing out of the Morris Minor range began in 1969. When the Abingdon contract ended, all Minor light commercial production was moved to BMC's Light Commercial Vehicle Division at Adderley Park in Birmingham, the former Wolseley and Morris-Commercial factory. With the need to clear the Cowley production lines for the introduction of the Austin Maxi and later the Morris Marina, it seemed logical to transfer Minor Traveller production to Adderley Park as well. The move occurred in July 1969, and assembly of the Traveller remained here, until the model was phased out in April 1971.

A factory review of the sales ledgers in September 1969 revealed that 204,279 Travellers had been made. Of these, 172,744 were home market models and 31,535 were export models, including those supplied to overseas assemblers as CKD (Completely Knocked Down) kits. Factory records from Adderley Park were destroyed after the plant closed. However, it is thought that the last batch of Travellers made at the plant, from November 1970 to April 1971, totalled 5705 cars, going by the chassis numbers. Taking this into account and adding some 10,000 for the period from September 1969 to November 1970, it is realistic to assume that the final production figure for the all models of the Minor Traveller was over 220,000 (see also table).

ABINGDON TRAVELLER PRODUCTION 1960-64	
1960	764
1961	1950
1962	2476
1963	4268
1964	1360
Total	10,818

PARTIAL TRAVELLER PRODUCTION FIGURES, FROM NUFFIELD, BMC AND BL RECORDS

	Home	Government	Export	Total for model	Total for calendar year
1959				17,482	17,482
1960	13,224	16	3564	16,804	16,804
1961	13,562	25	2048	15,635	15,635
1962, standard	1083	2	633	1718	
1962, De Luxe	11,293	5	883	12,181	13,899
1963, standard	628	14	459	1101	
1963, De Luxe	12,134	3	526	12,663	13,764
1964, standard	426	22	588	1036	
1964, De Luxe	15,536	44	467	16,047	17,083
1965, standard	246	12	595	853	
1965, De Luxe	10,743	79	478	11,300	12,153
1966, standard	308	7	717	1032	
1966, De Luxe	10,655	117	415	11,187	12,219
1967	11,566	215	1072	12,853	12,853
1968	11,910	556	1019	13,485	13,485
1969	7832	583	1152	9567	9567
1970	8606	729	727	10,062	10,062
1971	3270	0	0	3270	3270
				168,276	168,276

BUILDING THE TRAVELLER

When the Millionth Minor was made in early 1961, Nuffield's publicity department stated that of the million cars, there were 86,537 Travellers. If this is roughly the equal of production to the end of 1960, there would have been some 52,000 Travellers from 1953 to 1958 inclusive, giving again a total of over 220,000. It is estimated that there were around 20,500 Series II Travellers from 1953 to 1956 (see also Appendix).

OVERSEAS PRODUCTION AND EXPORTS

Production of the Morris Minor Traveller was mainly confined to the UK plants described above. Most Travellers were exported as complete vehicles to the dealer network throughout the world. Like the rest of the range, some specifications relating to left-hand drive fittings, lighting, and heating arrangements were changed for specific overseas markets. Actual assembly of Travellers was very restricted in overseas assembly plants, with most electing to concentrate on production of saloon, tourer, and light commercial models. Recent research has thrown some light on one of the major European assemblers, Molenaar, the Dutch Morris importer based at Amersfoort. Careful analysis of internal factory records, including sales books, has confirmed that

Recent research has revealed that as part of their prolific output of Morris Minors, Molenaar assembled some Traveller models from CKD kits.

Supplied in primer, this Dutch-assembled Traveller was painted using Sikkens paint and originally finished in Almond Green.

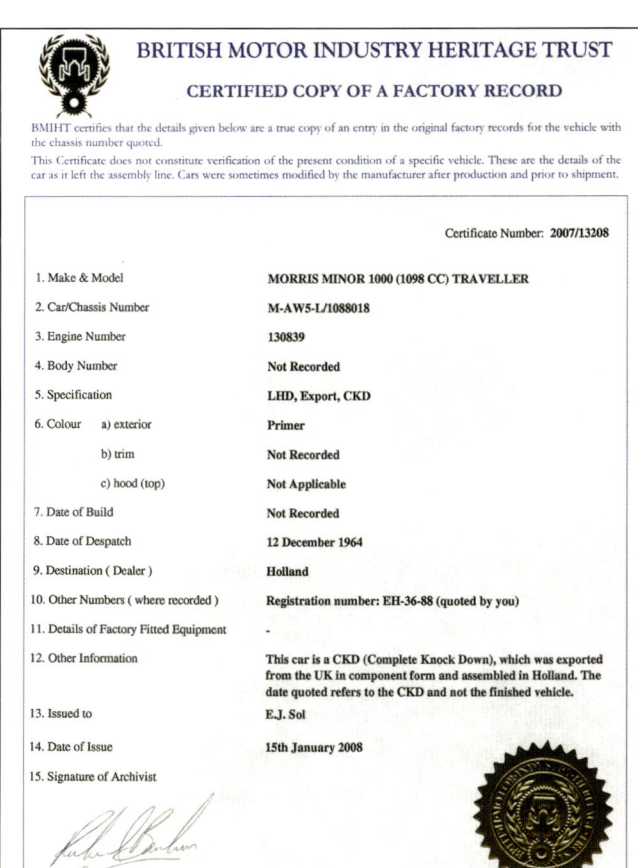

Molenaar did indeed assemble CKD Travellers.

Between January 1959 and March 1965, 245 Travellers were despatched from the UK in CKD form. The records show that the Travellers were usually despatched in batches of five, with sequential chassis numbers. They arrived at the plant in special crates which could be flat-packed when empty, ready for return to the UK. The CKD vehicles were supplied in primer and finished by Molenaar in standard BMC paint colours though using Sikkens paint. Two of the Dutch CKD Travellers are known to have survived and both

Jan Sol has diligently researched the history of his rare CKD Traveller built at Amersfoort.

Travellers were later exported as complete vehicles to Holland. This vehicle was bought new in 1968 and is still with the same owner.

exhibit the classic tell-tale sign of this type of assembly – the welded bar on either side of the battery box, where the top and bottom half of the bulkhead were joined together. Other features including locally-sourced components, such as Staalglas windows and Philips lighting, add confirmation of the Dutch origins. Not all Travellers supplied to Dutch customers were assembled by Molenaar. After 1965 when Morris Minor assembly ended in Holland, a small number of vehicles were directly imported from the UK.

SOUTH AFRICAN TRAVELLERS

In South Africa, the Motor Assemblies plant was one of the earliest plants to tackle the assembly of Traveller CKD models. In 1955, two prototype Series II CKD Travellers were assembled. The enterprise did not receive universal approval, and a further two years elapsed before an additional dozen Morris Minor 1000 Travellers were built. On this occasion there was a more favourable response, which led to a more substantial undertaking. This resulted in 690 Morris Minor 1000 948cc Travellers being built in the period from 1959 to 1962. A characteristic of the CKD South African Travellers is that most of those assembled were built to standard rather than De Luxe specification.

SOUTH AFRICAN TRAVELLER PRODUCTION 1955-62	
1955	2
1956	0
1957	12
1958	0
1959	295
1960	227
1961	156
1962	12
Total	704

A South African CKD Traveller undergoing restoration. Note the blanking plae in the trafficator aperture,

A CKD Traveller which was assembled at the Durban plant in South Africa in 1959, it now resides in the Eastern Cape. Note additional 'white' lamp for flashing indicators!

'Australian' Morris Minor 1000 which was imported from the UK in the 1960s. Finished in Silverpine Green with a Chamois interior with green piping, it is strikingly different to UK specification paint and trim options.

The colour scheme adopted when this vehicle was restored is indicative of how Australian built Travellers may have looked.

Unchanged 948cc engine is still providing economical motoring 'Down Under'.

TRAVELLERS IN AUSTRALIA AND NEW ZEALAND

Australia was a major market for the export of Morris Minors in the early years of production. With the establishment of Nuffield (Australia) Pty Ltd at Zetland, New South Wales, production of a wide range of Nuffield vehicles progressed rapidly. Morris Minors featured prominently, with saloon and tourer models being the most prolific. Serious consideration was given to adding Morris Minor Travellers to the list. CKD kits were despatched from the UK, but according to former employees at the Zetland plant, they did not become a regular part of production. In fact their demise has passed into local folklore, with stories of the Traveller ash frames being cast aside and eventually burned! Unsurprisingly there are relatively few Morris Minor Travellers in Australia. Those that do exist were either fully built-up Travellers exported to Australian Nuffield dealers when new, or second-hand cars imported from the UK post-production.

In neighbouring New Zealand, a similar policy decision was taken at the Dominion Motor Company. Though a wide range of Nuffield vehicles were assembled and Morris Minor production continued long after it ceased in the UK, no Morris Minor Travellers were ever assembled there. Demand for Morris Minor models far exceeded supply, particularly in the late 1950s. A combination of import restrictions, high sales prices, and high petrol taxes created long waiting lists for new vehicles. Contemporary advertising by Nuffield dealerships highlighted the opportunities to acquire vehicles from the UK. As a result, some Travellers were supplied under the 'No Remittance' licensing scheme. This system favoured relatively well-off purchasers who had private funds held overseas with which to buy their imported vehicle.

TRAVELLERS IN NORTH AMERICA

Right from the start of Morris Minor production, there were high expectations that the North American markets would account for a sizeable proportion of overall sales. Initially this proved to be the case, with Series MM saloon (sedan) and tourer (convertible) models selling well between 1949 and 1952. The innovative features of the compact Morris Minor caught the attention of sizeable numbers of US and Canadian motorists. However, by the time the Morris Minor Station Wagon became available for export in late 1953, sales in both the USA and Canada were on the decline. Reaction to the Series II models with the 803cc overhead valve engine was less favourable, as can be judged from the road test reports quoted in chapter 2, and this was reflected in a downturn in sales. In the USA, only 1439 Series II models were sold in 1953, and by the following year this had slumped to an alarming 430 cars. A similar trend was emerging in Canada, where 3144 Series II models were sold in 1953 and only 278 in 1954. By contrast, total Series MM sales in Canada during the preceding four years had reached a creditable 14,539.

Renewed interest in the Morris Minor range emerged, following the introduction of the Morris 1000 models in 1956. An expansion of the dealer network in the USA, fuelled by MG's success, helped to increase customer confidence, and this combined with a much more positive attitude towards the 948cc Morris Minor resulted in healthy sales of 39,230 between 1957 and 1960. This helped push the USA to second place behind Australia for export sales when BMC reviewed total sales in November 1960 (see table below). Although sales of Traveller models increased, the vast majority of sales were of two-door saloons (sedans). Then the sales of imported cars in the USA fell drastically in 1960. By 1964, sales to the USA had declined to a mere 212 for all Morris cars. The boom, such as it was, was well and truly over, and when strict emission controls were introduced in the USA in 1968, sales of new Minors effectively ceased.

A nicely preserved Traveller in the New World.

NORTH AMERICAN TRAVELLERS

Specifications for North American Travellers differed slightly from UK models. The main differences were:
Flashing indicators were fitted instead of semaphore indicators, with clear indicator lenses at the front and red lenses at the rear, also on cars later than 1963.
Revised lighting including changed bulbs in 7 inch headlamp units and Lucas 301 dip right 36/36w on Series II models.
Laminated windscreen.
Induction heaters.
Twin wind-tone horns.
Changed dip switch arrangement, with special bracket.
On Morris Minor 1000 models:
Sealed beam headlamps; the later type for American markets was identified by the number 2 moulded into the lens.
From 1964, US models were fitted with 10ME engines which had positive crankcase ventilation and incorporated a specially designed breather control valve.

BUILDING THE TRAVELLER

The world's BIGGEST small car buy!

MORRIS '1000'

More living per gallon...
Never before has a "small" family car been so universally acclaimed — and, so <u>enthusiastically</u>!

Available in 2-Door Sedan, 4-Door Sedan, Convertible and Station Wagon Models
Every new Morris car carries a TWELVE MONTHS' WARRANTY on parts

In the years since production ended, there has been renewed interest in Morris Minors and Traveller models in North America. Good sound right-hand drive examples have been imported from the UK by enthusiastic individuals keen to have a British 'Woodie' as part of their classic car collection. Some have been modified and modernised, others have formed the basis for 'custom cars'. Reassuringly, an increasing number of original LHD Travellers are being restored, using wood replacement kits supplied from the UK.

America, home of the 'Woodie', marketed the Traveller models as 'Station Wagons' as this leaflet, dated 1958, from a New York distributor shows.

Looking slightly out of place against a backdrop of skyscrapers, one wonders how the modest Traveller copes with New York driving conditions.

TOP TEN EXPORT MARKETS FOR ALL MORRIS MINORS FROM 1948 TO NOVEMBER 1960

		Percentage of export	Percentage of production of 987,364 cars
Australia	101,246	21.11%	10.25%
USA	52,431	10.93%	5.31%
Eire	35,492	7.40%	3.59%
South Africa	34,639	7.22%	3.51%
New Zealand	34,216	7.14%	3.47%
Canada	29,538	6.16%	2.99%
Sweden	25,375	5.29%	2.57%
Holland	20,356	4.25%	2.06%
Malaya	16,405	3.42%	1.66%
Denmark	14,213	2.96%	1.44%
Total of above	363,911	75.89%	36.86%
Total of all exports	479,525	100%	48.57%

Minor Travellers retain their appeal in many of the export markets and countries where they were built. Interest continues from classic car enthusiasts anxious to acquire 'Woodies' from the UK, as does the willingness to undertake complete restoration using imported ash frames.

MORRIS MINOR TRAVELLER – THE COMPLETE COMPAION

CHAPTER 6
DANISH SPECIAL: MORRIS 1000 COMBI

One of the most unusual variants of the Traveller was the Morris 1000 Combi and Super Combi modified by the Danish importers DOMI (Dansk Oversøisk Motor Industri) based at Glostrup near Copenhagen. This company had a long-established association with Morris Motors and later BMC. An assembly plant had been built after World War Two but unfortunately, it was largely destroyed in a disastrous fire in 1951. A new, more modern and sophisticated plant was built, and a variety of vehicles were assembled from CKD (Completely Knocked Down) kits in the years that followed. These included some Morris Minors, especially light commercial vehicles. Other models were supplied fully built-up to the Danish market, and these included Minor Travellers.

For many overseas markets, there were some variations in the specifications of the vehicles exported there. Some were related to prevailing climatic conditions. In Scandinavia, more powerful heaters were fitted as standard in order to cope with the harsher winters. In Denmark, safety legislation introduced in 1957 prevented the use of the traditional Morris motif fitted to the bonnet on post-1953 vehicles. Instead, the earlier simple chrome strip used on the Series MM models and on light commercial vehicles was used on all later Minors.

Some Danish Minor models varied in other respects too. In case of the commercials, the separate chassis allowed for variation in body design. In order to increase the load carrying space of the van, a special Danish-designed rear body was fitted to the standard LCV chassis. It featured an extended roofline, at the level of the cab roof, which increased carrying capacity. It incorporated differently-profiled rear wheel arches, and a single side-opening rear door, with a one-piece window. There were rear quarter bumpers. Inside, the rear load area was separated from the cab by a substantial wire mesh screen. These vans were used mainly by small private businesses. This model, known as the 'De Luxe' van, is now particularly rare. Only two are known to exist and both are still in Denmark. This body was offered

A Minor Combi might indeed come in handy for taking the grain to the mill or the flour back home again.

DANISH SPECIAL: MORRIS 1000 COMBI

Danish assemblers DOMI produced this unique Minor known as the De Luxe van. The portholes are not original.

at first on the 803cc split-screen model and continued with the 948cc Morris 1000 models, but was discontinued in the late 1950s, perhaps because the Combi became available.

The Combi was specifically aimed at exploiting the potential for commercial use of the Morris 1000 Traveller in the Danish market. It was prompted by local legislation (see sidebar) which allowed variation in taxable status by the simple expedient of removing the rear side windows and replacing them with metal panels. This enabled the Traveller to be marketed as a commercial vehicle, with the advantage of a reduction in the amount of Purchase Tax payable. The savings were substantial, and provided a golden opportunity for DOMI's marketing department to promote these vehicles in Denmark. In consequence, sales of these particular models proved highly popular, and second-hand examples were even bought by discerning Norwegian and Swedish customers.

The Combi designation was presumably an attempt at reflecting the possibility of dual use, but it was the price tag which proved most popular. Understandably there was considerable interest in the Combi, as the discount provided welcome relief to Danish customers who were used to paying exorbitantly high Purchase Tax on all cars. However, the savings did come with some strings attached. In Denmark, those using the Combi Travellers for business could avoid paying Purchase Tax altogether, but then had to register the vehicles for commercial use only, and were allocated distinctive yellow number plates. Vehicles with yellow plates were restricted to use during the working week, and any infringement of the conditions resulted in fines. An alternative half-way stage was the part yellow, part black number plates,

called by the Danes 'parrot plates' as they were multi-coloured, which offered a 50 per cent rebate on the tax, yet still allowed the vehicle to be fitted with rear seats, and to be used for private motoring at weekends. The rear side windows remained blanked out.

The cost savings available on the Combi models were heavily promoted.

In 1961, the number of Morris 1000 cars sold in Denmark was 1561 (for a 15th place in the sales statistic, where the VW Beetle was first with 14,625 sales...) but the combined sales of all Morris vans was 1359, most of which must have been Minors, including Combis. Production of the Morris 1000 Combi continued for several years and when the larger 1098cc engine was introduced in 1962, the designation of this Danish Traveller changed to Morris 1000 Super Combi. The Combi model remained popular in Denmark until the late 1960s.

IN FEBRUARY 1960, THE FOLLOWING PRICES WERE QUOTED FOR THE DIFFERENT VERSIONS OF THE MINOR 1000 IN DENMARK:

Model	Price in Kroner	Equivalent in £
Two-door saloon, black plate, full Purchase Tax	15,138	£783
Traveller, black plate, full Purchase Tax	Ca. 18,500	£957
Combi Traveller, 'parrot plate', half Purchase Tax	13,694	£708
Combi Traveller, yellow plate, no Purchase Tax	9725	£503

DECEMBER 1968 PRICES FOR THE SALOON, NORMAL TRAVELLER AND THE COMBI TRAVELLER WERE AS FOLLOWS:

Model	Price in Kroner	Equivalent in £
Two-door saloon, black plate, full Purchase Tax	16,994	£944
Traveller, black plate, full Purchase Tax	21,646	£1203
Combi Traveller, 'parrot plate', half Purchase Tax	15,995	£889
Combi Traveller, yellow plate, no Purchase Tax	10,452	£581

Shortly after, the rules were changed and the 'parrot plates' were abolished.

DOMI publicity shot of the Combi from the 1960s. It has neither over-riders nor external mirrors but does have repeater indicators at the top of the B-posts, as required by Danish law.

DANISH SPECIAL: MORRIS 1000 COMBI

DOMI publicity often featured the standard Traveller and the Combi together. Illustrations were usually taken from home market brochures but were retouched to show left-hand drive.

The specifications of the Combi models mirrored those of other export models in terms of mechanical components. The only difference was that the rear side windows were replaced by the full-length metal side panels. These fitted neatly into the original ash top rail and the outer channel on the wood waist rail, originally designed to accommodate the sliding windows. Once secured in position, the panels were sealed with light-coloured putty. The original rear doors with windows were retained, to allow rearward visibility for the driver, and to allow adequate light into the rear compartment. The rear doors retained all the usual fittings, including the locating arms to secure the doors in the open position.

Panelling on the inside of the body was necessary to avoid substantial damage occurring when loading and unloading, both to the upper metal side panels and to the lower aluminium inserts fitted to the ash frame. The extra panelling was fitted in two sections to each side. In the case of the top section, the inner part of the window channel was used to locate the inner panels which were usually made of hardboard. Shaped lower panels were fitted below the inner waist rail on both sides. They were contoured to fit around the rear wheel arches and at the forward edges next to the B-posts, and extended downwards to enclose fully the area adjacent to the rear seat. Another unusual feature of the Combi was the retention of a full-length roof lining, identical to that used in standard Traveller models. Given the robust nature of commercial enterprise and the rather fragile nature of the roof lining material, it does seem odd that this was not replaced with a more solid one-piece, covered panel. Another interesting change on later Combi models was the decision to cover the hardboard panelling with a durable light-coloured fabric, similar in colour and texture to the roof lining.

The Combi models which were exclusively used as commercial vehicles had some additional features. An extended wood platform, with wood supports, was fitted to provide a continuous level surface in the rear loading area. This extended forward to the back of the cab, where a metal-framed wire mesh partition was positioned. Two types were available: a full-width partition which extended right across the back of the front seats, and a half-width one which fitted just behind the driver's seat. In this guise the Combi models

Inevitably, after 1968 Danish publicity used the British Leyalnd and DOMI logos together, as DOMI gradually took over the agencies for all the BL brands.

This preserved Combi now carries white-on-black number plates but still has the blanked-off rear side windows. Again no overriders, indicating standard specification.

were just as effective as any other Minor van, and the wheel arches remained uncovered, as they were on the van. The floor of the load area was also uncovered.

Not many of these vehicles survive, and many that do have been converted into original specification Travellers, with side windows and Traveller rear seats, vinyl covered trim panels, and a storage area behind the rear seat. It would seem that owning a more valuable standard specification Traveller far outweighs the rarity value and interest generated by what was a unique specification vehicle which exploited the potential for dual-purpose use. At the time of writing, just three unconverted Combi models are known to survive in Denmark.

Rear views of the Combi model showing the metal inserts in place of the normal Traveller side windows.

DANISH SPECIAL: MORRIS 1000 COMBI

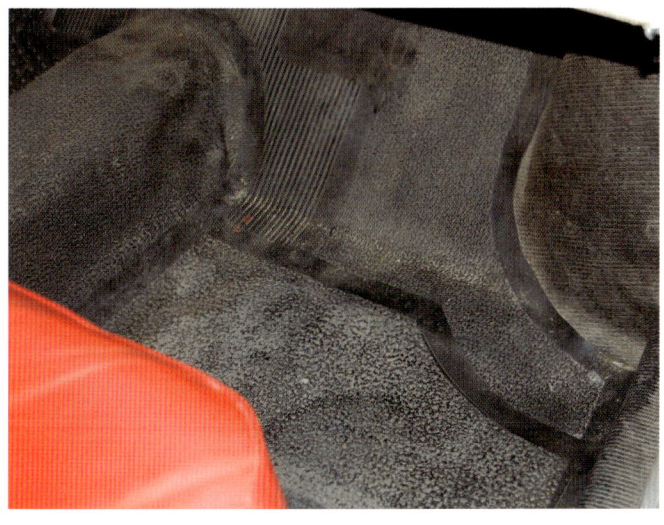

Rear view showing the owner's name sign-written to meet the precise requirements of Danish legislation, together with the permitted weights (below).

The original moulded rubber floor covering on this Combi has survived remarkably well. Interestingly this version extends to cover the front inner wheel arches.

The original Traveller headlining was retained in the Combi. Note the mounting bracket for the safety partition which had to be fitted if the vehicle was used for commercial purposes only.

Interior panels were covered with a light coloured vinyl on later models, as shown here.

Interior panelling was quite basic with hardboard sheets used to line the inside.

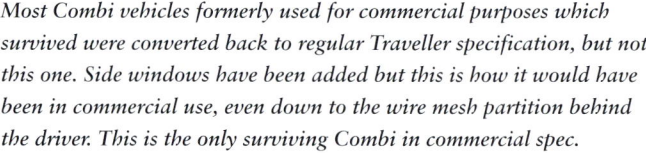

Most Combi vehicles formerly used for commercial purposes which survived were converted back to regular Traveller specification, but not this one. Side windows have been added but this is how it would have been in commercial use, even down to the wire mesh partition behind the driver. This is the only surviving Combi in commercial spec.

'DANELAW'

Rules and regulations governing the registration and use of commercial vehicles in Denmark were extremely complicated. Due in part to the tax savings available, they were also carefully monitored, and any violation resulted in severe penalties being imposed, including payment of the full amount of Purchase Tax. Part of the monitoring process involved the issuing of colour-coded number plates. These were intended to indicate the permissible use, whether personal or commercial, of a particular vehicle.

Three different types of number plates were issued and all of these could be found on Minor Travellers in Denmark. A Traveller bought in Denmark as a standard vehicle with sliding windows, was designated as a 'station car' (the 'Danish' term for estate car) and was registered with black enamelled number plates with white figures. Vehicles registered with these plates were not subject to any restrictions in use, but attracted the full amount of Purchase Tax. For a car in the Minor 1000 price class, under the 1957 tariff this tax was set at 3545 Danish Kroner (around £183 at the time) on the first 5000 Kroner (£258) of basic price, and 95 per cent on any additional amount, up to a total of 10,000 Kroner. The tax payable on cars in this class was typically around 80 per cent of basic price, and the percentage rate rose progressively on more expensive cars.

Minor 1000 Combi models on the other hand were issued with different coloured plates. There were two types. A yellow plate with black figures was issued for those vehicles which were exclusively used for business purposes. Such vehicles were exempt from Purchase Tax, but were restricted to commercial use. A saving of between 44 per cent and 50 per cent on the normal purchase price was possible. In 1961 when the white Combi featured in this chapter was purchased and first registered on yellow plates, the saving on the normal purchase price was 44 per cent. By 1968, the possible savings for a similar vehicle had risen to over 50 per cent.

However, the restrictions on use were severe. At first it was impossible to purchase a yellow-plate Combi unless you could prove, beyond doubt, that you were a bona fide business or trades person, and the vehicle was going to be used exclusively for commercial purposes.

Even when the purchase was authorised, the restrictions on use were quite off-putting. You could only carry a passenger, if needed to help load or unload cargo. The vehicle could not be used for personal or recreational use, and a license had to be obtained from The Ministry of Public Works for every trip abroad, if a passenger was needed to help with the cargo!

Other regulations specific to the vehicle were rigidly enforced. The installation of windows, rear seats, or a sunroof, was not permitted, and there had to be a fixed barrier between the driver and the load compartment. Finally, the name of the owner had to be sign-written somewhere on the external panels of the vehicle in a contrasting colour in letters 10cm (4in) high. However the use of gold or silver lettering was not allowed!

The second type of registration plate used on Combi models was introduced in 1957 and was called a 'parrot plate' (*papegøjeplade*), with a black letter on a yellow background (two letters from 1958) indicating the local registration area, and the number in white figures on a black background. This special plate indicated that such a vehicle was allowed dual use. Parrot-plated cars were subject to fewer restrictions on use, and rear seats were usually fitted. The amount of Purchase Tax was halved. In consequence, the retail price was reduced by between 22 and 26 per cent compared to a standard production Traveller.

Anyone could purchase a parrot-plate Combi model, but, to quote a 1960 Danish publication, 'in certain sectors of society, a degree of moral courage is required to announce that you have bought a van.' Other restrictions still applied, thus side windows or a sun roof could not be fitted, and special permission still had to be sought, if the car was to be taken abroad, with passengers. When transporting passengers, the vehicle documents had to be carried by the driver, and a special MOT test was required for approval to carry passengers. As with the Combi models used exclusively for commercial purposes, the owner's name had to be sign-written on the parrot-plated vehicles.

The regulations did not end there. If a Combi model was sold and its designated use was changed, then a recalculation of the tax payable was undertaken, and new registration plates were issued. If this was done during the first 500km, the full tax reduction would have to be repaid. Thereafter this was recalculated on a sliding scale, depending on the age and estimated value of the vehicle.

The white Combi which has survived in remarkable condition has undergone two such recalculations, first in 1967 when a sum of 896 Danish Kroner (say £50) was paid. At this point the yellow plates were replaced with parrot plates. In 1971, when the owner wanted to upgrade the car again and have black plates issued, the value of the vehicle had reduced sufficiently for no additional tax payments to be made. The only fees payable were for the new plates, and the administration costs in issuing new documentation.

CHAPTER 7
MILITARY AND POLICE TRAVELLERS

In the UK, much later registration plates on Morris Minor Travellers, like on this ex army vehicle, are a useful clue that they may have been supplied as special contract vehicles to the armed services.

To the casual observer, the Morris Minor may seem an odd choice to add to a fleet of Military vehicles. Yet sizeable numbers of Minor 1000 Travellers were commissioned by the British Army, the Royal Navy, and the Royal Air Force in the late 1960s. They were deployed in a variety of ways, with the principal uses being transport of goods, equipment, and personnel. In total 2088 Morris Minors were commissioned and deployed to various bases in Britain, mainland Europe, and other overseas destinations, including Cyprus and Malta. Some production figures for Government contract vehicles are quoted in chapter 5.

ARMY
The British Army was the most prolific of all the Armed Forces in its use of Minor Travellers. Though a few contracts were placed in the early 1960s, the vast majority were placed during the final years of production, between 1966 and 1971. Most of the Travellers had right-hand drive and were

MILITARY AND POLICE TRAVELLERS

When in Service the Travellers carried various insignia to denote the arm of the service to which they had been deployed.

destined for use on army bases in Britain. However at that time, the British Army had considerable overseas commitments too. One of the largest was the post-war deployment of the British Army on the Rhine (BAOR) in Germany. Part of the vehicle support included contracts totalling orders for 747 left-hand drive Morris 1000 Travellers.

All of the vehicles were assigned their own unique military identity and carried insignia denoting the arm of the service, and the unit to which they had been deployed. Some vehicles had transfers applied to the bonnet, and many had special heraldic signs fitted on the front bumper and rear doors. Vehicles assigned to NATO duties usually had a transfer of the British national flag on the bonnet and rear door. In addition each vehicle had its own data plate. In case of Army vehicles, this was located in the engine bay and was secured on the right-hand side of the bulkhead. As well as the chassis number of the vehicle, the unique military registration number, referred to as the vehicle number, was stamped on the plate along with the contract number, code number, and the vehicle designation. For Morris Minor Travellers this was 'Car Utility 4 x 2 Morris 1000'.

The Army Travellers had many distinguishing features, the most notable of which was the paint and interior trim colour combination. The vast majority of the Army Travellers were supplied in a deep Bronze Green exterior paint finish. However, once in service considerable numbers were subsequently over-painted in Army regulation matt mid-olive green. Others assigned to specific duties had unique liveries. The most striking of these were the vehicles deployed to the Royal Army Ordinance Corps for use as Bomb Disposal vehicles. Apart from the roof-mounted signs which highlighted their role, these vehicles sported contrast-colour front and rear wings which were painted bright red. 81 Travellers were despatched to duties in the tropics, and some may have been painted white or have had white roof panels. Those on the UK mainland which were specifically used as staff cars were painted black.

The internal specifications for the army vehicles differed in many respects from standard Morris 1000 Travellers on sale to the general public. Presumably in an effort to reduce costs, some subtle changes were introduced, particularly to the interior trim. Travellers supplied as part of the early contracts had light green trim. However, in keeping with other special contract vehicles, the door cards had a plain vinyl finish, as opposed to the heat-formed fluted finish of the standard production vehicles. The side trim panels next to the rear seat did not have arm rests. A hard-wearing contoured rubber mat was supplied as the interior floor covering, however the wood boards in the rear loading area remained exposed, and on early models the inner rear wheel arches were painted body colour. On models supplied under later contracts, different interior colours were used, including Black and Autumn Leaf (brown), and some models were supplied with De Luxe specification door cards. Some even had the rear inner wheel arches covered in matching vinyl!

The Army Travellers also had some special equipment. All

Finding pictures of Armed Service vehicles 'in action' is a rare occurrence. Here an Army Bomb Disposal Traveller is deployed on a mission to defuse an unexploded bomb.

Following restoration this particular ex Army Traveller was allocated a period registration number. When in service it was based with the Royal Electrical and Mechanical Engineers (REME) at Aborfield, England. It was used by the Medical Officer and the Padre.

One particular Army Traveller has been preserved in original condition at the RAF Museum at Cosford. It too retains many original features: original rubber floor covering, fire extinguisher mounting point, and a 1098cc engine repainted in 'duck egg' blue with an additional plate attached to denote what work had been undertaken to overhaul it in the workshops! This vehicle was presented to the Museum in 1986 by Number 34 Base Workshops (REME, Donnington, England).

were supplied with a fire extinguisher. This was a standard Ministry of Defence issue, and came complete with a mounting bracket. It was usual for this to be located on the inner wheel arch in the passenger side foot well underneath the parcel shelf, but some were mounted on the transmission tunnel in front of the gear lever, while others were mounted on the upper part of the wooden cover panel on the passenger side B-post. Some individual vehicles were fitted with revised seat runners which allowed for easier and quicker seat adjustment. On reflection this was a sensible modification, given that a number of drivers of different sizes might use the vehicles. An added bonus was that access to the rear seat was improved.

Mechanically, the Morris 1000 Travellers supplied to the Armed Forces were mostly standard specification vehicles. Occasionally a few changes were necessary in order to cope with particular circumstances. For instance, some of the Travellers which were used in tropical climates had a revised three-core radiator for improved cooling. Considerable numbers of the Army vehicles were supplied with a low-compression version of the tried and tested 1098cc A-series engine.

MILITARY AND POLICE TRAVELLERS

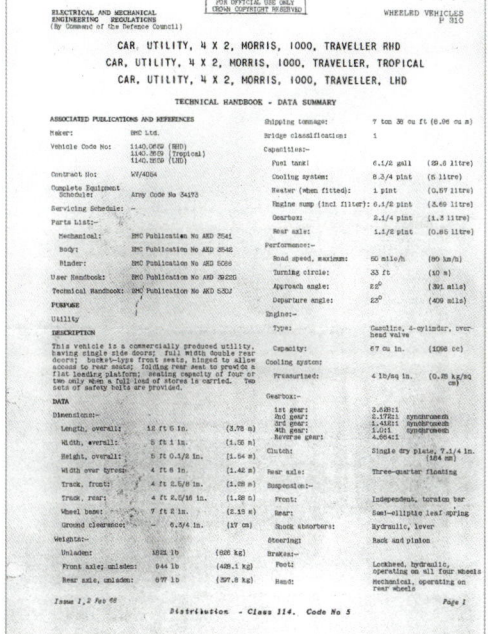

MORRIS MINOR TRAVELLER – THE COMPLETE COMPANION

RAF Travellers were used extensively for the transport of goods and personnel. Like all military vehicles they were disposed of at special auctions. This model has had a new lease of life since being decommissioned.

Sporting its RAF registration number and finished in RAF Blue this Traveller still retains many of the original internal features of the Travellers supplied on Contract to the armed forces.

ROYAL AIR FORCE

The Royal Air Force found the Morris Minor 1000 Traveller to be ideal for use on bases at home and abroad. It proved its worth as a versatile practical vehicle, which was easy to maintain, and for which parts were readily available should they be needed. A total of 253 Travellers were commissioned by the RAF, and of these about half a dozen were deployed to Cyprus. In keeping with tradition, these vehicles were painted in the familiar RAF Blue-Grey colour. However, some variation did occur when the vehicles were specifically assigned to airfield duties. Some panels were painted yellow, presumably to make the vehicles more visible from the air as well as on the ground.

So far as the general specifications of the RAF Travellers were concerned, they differed very little from those supplied to the Army. Trim options were the same in style, but differed in colour. To complement the Blue-Grey paint, interior trim was dark blue. Data plates were positioned differently on the RAF models. Though they were much smaller than those used on Army Travellers they were more obvious, due to the fact that they were attached to the passenger side glove box lid.

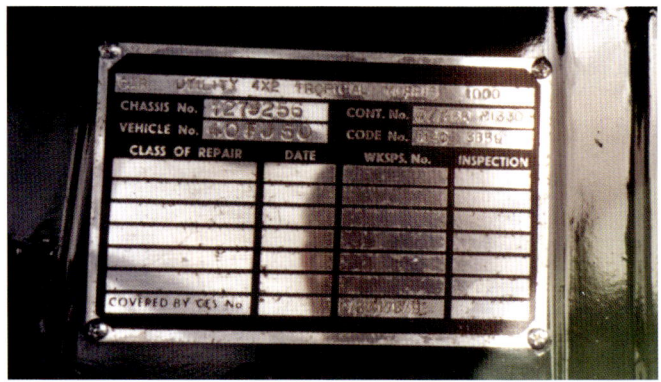

Different style identification plates were used on Military Travellers. Army Travellers had a large plate fitted in the engine bay. The one illustrated is for a 'Tropical' Traveller. The RAF Identification plates were more discreetly proportioned and were fitted to the glove box lid.

MILITARY AND POLICE TRAVELLERS

Large numbers of Morris Minor Travellers were deployed by the British Army on the Rhine (BAOR) in Germany. This ex-BAOR Traveller now registered in Holland has been converted to run on LPG. It still exhibits many of the original features of the Army specifications including painted wheel arches, uncovered boards in the rear floor area, and plain door panels.

ROYAL NAVY

Of the three Armed Services, the Royal Navy commissioned the fewest Morris Minor Travellers. Only 64 vehicles were acquired, but the range of duties to which they were assigned was wide ranging. As well as seeing service in Royal Navy dockyards, a number were used by HM Customs and the Coastguard Service. Some vehicles were taken on board ships sailing to far-flung destinations, and then used as regular transport in ports of call. Unlike the Army and the Royal Air Force where the vehicles were acquired under contracts which specified particular features, the Royal Navy Travellers appear to have been mostly De Luxe models which were painted in the traditional 'Navy' blue or in Black. Relatively few of the vehicles are known to have survived. No service records have so far been located. However, it is known that like their Army and Air Force counterparts, they were assigned military registration numbers, and remained in service until the mid 1970s.

Considerable interest remains in the Military Travellers, most of which were disposed of at auction following their

MORRIS MINOR TRAVELLER – THE COMPLETE COMPANION

There are no service records of the Royal Navy Travellers. This rare survivor, painted black, was assigned to duties with the Coastguard Service in conjunction with the Custom and Excise Department. It survives but not in the condition shown here.

decommissioning from active service. In Britain, the major disposal point in the 1970s was at the Royal Army Ordinance Corps's Ordinance and Storage and Disposal Depot at Ruddington in Nottinghamshire (now part of Rushcliffe Country Park and the National Transport Heritage Trust). Most of the vehicles were sent to auction after five years service, or when they failed to meet the stringent requirements for continued service. At the time they were much sought after, as they were known to have been well maintained in the various military workshops.

Once sold as surplus, these ex-military vehicles were registered with civilian number plates. Though some more recent finds and some restoration projects have been allocated age-related registration plates appropriate to their date of manufacture, many of the vehicles which were registered in the 1970s have plates which indicate the year in which the individual vehicle was first registered, after military service. They are a useful indicator that the vehicle may have an interesting history. Most of the surviving vehicles are to be found in Britain and Holland. Though many have been restored, a considerable number remain true to the original specification, and provide a valuable record of the particular characteristics of the special contract military Minors.

In Germany, most of the left-hand drive BAOR vehicles were disposed of at sales held in Mönchen-Gladbach. Over 200 were sold to Holland. Two Dutch companies were responsible for the eventual resale of these vehicles. One, Antique and Classic Cars, was based near Haarlem. Before sale the vehicles were re-registered with Dutch civilian registration numbers, and the specification was amended to meet local requirements. Lighting regulations forced a change to the headlamps, and for testing purposes the brake fluid reservoir had to be mounted on the bulkhead. The ex-army Minors proved popular in Holland, particularly as relatively few Travellers were assembled as part of Minor production by the Dutch Molenaar company (see chapter 5). As in Britain, many of the vehicles provided reliable transport for many years for their civilian owners, and some survive in the hands of enthusiastic Morris Minor Club Nederland (MMCN) members.

POLICE VEHICLES

Within the armed forces, the Ministry of Defence Police also used Minor Travellers. Though supplied on contract, these did not follow the normal convention in terms of the livery adopted by different arms of the service. Instead these vehicles were usually painted black, and were easily distinguished by Police signs and associated external equipment. In 'Civvy Street', various Police forces also commissioned Travellers as part of their vehicle fleets in the early 1960s. At this time the vehicles were usually painted black, and most were used as transport for officers in supervisory roles. However, there are recorded instances where Minor Travellers were used by CID officers, Police photographers, and Police dog handlers.

In 1967, changes in operational duties within the Police forces throughout the United Kingdom caused a rethink in the deployment of personnel and the use of vehicles. A long-term trial for what was to become 'Unit Beat Policing' was

Travellers were also deployed on Military bases for the use of the Ministry of Defence Military Police

MILITARY AND POLICE TRAVELLERS

held in Lancashire. It proved successful and the programme was rolled out nationwide. Panda cars became a familiar sight, and Morris Minors were pressed into service along with a variety of other marques. Minor two-door saloons proved popular, though a number of forces, including Edinburgh, Derbyshire, Leicestershire, and the West Midlands Police, supplemented their fleet with Travellers.

A key feature of these vehicles was their distinctive livery. While not uniform across all forces, a common feature for many Panda Cars was the Bermuda Blue colour adopted for most of the body. Contrast in the colour scheme was provided by painting the roof forward of the B-posts, as well as the doors, Police White. Police signs were added to the doors, and an illuminated sign was added to the roof. Some forces, such as Leicestershire, used a variation on this theme with the Traveller models. The contrasting white stripe, which extended over the roof and onto the doors, was only half the width of the door.

The changes in specification did not end there. In order to access the roof-mounted police sign on two-door saloons, a special zipped headlining was fitted. If some of the anecdotes shared amongst serving officers are true, this became a welcome repository for packed lunches, as well as the occasional pasty or pie!

Other distinguishing features of the Police Panda vehicles included extra strengthening in the base of the driver's seat, and the fitting of an alternator to provide additional charging to the electrical system. Both items were added to the specification in anticipation of the heavy usage the vehicles were expected to have. The use of Morris Minors for Police work was widespread in the late 1960s. The Metropolitan Police had four-door saloons finished in Trafalgar Blue for senior officers, and Buckinghamshire Police used Travellers, usually painted black, as supervision cars, mainly for the use of Sergeants and Inspectors. While two-door saloons remained the most popular, they were not the only Minors used by the Constabulary. Minor vans were used by Police Dog handlers, and by scene of crime officers in forces such as Hertfordshire and Durham. The use of Minors as Police vehicles was not confined to Britain either. The Bermuda Police force used them and included Travellers as part of their fleet.

The Traveller proved eminently suitable for a variety of Police activities – providing transport as staff cars for Senior Officers, Police photographers, scene of crime officers and even dog handlers and their canine companions. Many police forces deployed Morris Minor Travellers in Panda style livery. This Traveller was used by the Leicestershire Force.

The use of Morris Minor Travellers was not confined to UK Police Forces. The Bermuda Police adopted this interesting livery for their Police Traveller.

The RN designation on the number plates indicates that these Military Police Travellers were assigned to the Royal Navy.

CHAPTER 8
WOODWORK – DISMANTLING

A new set of wood definitely required.

Most, if not all, of the tools you will need.

One of the many virtues of the basic design of the Morris Minor is the ease of access to all components for general maintenance and when required, restoration. This is true of all models in the range. However in the case of the Traveller, many would-be restorers are deterred from taking on a full restoration, because of the perceived intricacies of the wood frame, or a genuine fear that it will prove too onerous or difficult to maintain, once it has been replaced. Others, lacking in confidence to tackle the replacement of all, or part, of the wood frame themselves, see it as the domain of the professional restorer with all the attendant costs. Such concerns, while not entirely unjustified, are familiar to Steve Foreman, managing director of the renowned Woodies Company of Chichester. With thirty years of experience of manufacturing ash frames and almost as many years fitting them, he has heard most of the queries and concerns and dealt with almost every conceivable practical problem. After having fitted wood frames to nearly one thousand Travellers, Steve and his son James, who is now an integral part of the family business, are eminently qualified to provide a comprehensive guide to all aspects of removing, replacing, and maintaining Traveller wood.

In the pages which follow, Steve and James prove beyond doubt that it is within the abilities of the competent home restorer to tackle the removal and replacement of all or part of the ash frame structure on the Minor Traveller. Steve through his lucid and informative text and James with clear precise photography, provide a comprehensive guide to each task involved. Key areas are identified and the correct sequence of activities is outlined, with helpful tips given along the way. In the process, many myths and pieces of misinformation which have been perpetuated through internet forums are dispelled, and improvements to the original design are identified and discussed. Steve's aim is to provide easily accessible information which will encourage existing and would-be Traveller owners to maintain and when necessary replace the wood on their vehicles. In so doing, he and James will help contribute to the continued use and preservation of vehicles, which have been their passion and livelihood for most of their lives.

From the outset, let it be clearly understood that what follows is not intended to be a definitive guide to budding concours restorers. It is specifically targeted information and guidance aimed at boosting the confidence of the majority of Traveller owners, while providing them with sufficient knowledge to enable them to achieve a professional standard of restoration. In the process, consideration will be given to the inherent faults of the original design, which led to weaknesses in the construction and ensuing wood rot, as well as rusting metalwork. Improvements will be outlined and incorporated, though it should be stressed that their inclusion will not cause any change to the outward appearance of the vehicle.

In adopting the format which follows, a reasonable level of competence and common sense has been assumed, so as to avoid a series of mind-numbing step-by-step instructions. In each section of the chapters which follow, sequenced tasks will be fully explained by Steve and, where appropriate, will be illustrated with relevant detailed photographs taken by James.

PREPARING FOR RESTORATION

Classic car restorations have been undertaken in a variety of locations. Depending on where in the world you live, it may be possible to carry out most tasks associated with the removal and replacement of Traveller wood out in the open. For most restorers though, a garage or at least a car port is a desirable option, with easy access to a reliable and safe power source being essential. A range of good quality tools will make the task much easier. As the assembly of the Traveller body is very basic, there is no need to embark on vast expenditure on specialist tools. A useful investment would be a power screwdriver, preferably the lightest and most powerful your budget will stretch to. For phase one of the restoration, the acquisition of a small grinder which can be fitted with ultra-thin cutting discs will prove invaluable. Apart from these items, a selection of spanners (AF and Whitworth), a variety of screwdrivers, a hammer, a chisel, and a good pair of mole grips will be required, but little else. Ever mindful of health and safety, a strong pair of boots or protective shoes, safety goggles, and protective gloves are always useful.

Two other less obvious items will be required. Patience… whether that applies to the restorer, the immediate family, or the neighbours, or all three is open to conjecture. The second is a digital camera. This may seem a surprising inclusion. The use of digital photography is useful for recording the progress of the restoration, and for creating additional provenance for the vehicle. However, for the inexperienced restorer it can provide an invaluable reminder to how things were before dismantling began. Given that years could elapse before they are put back together, vital reference photographs of items such as window channel fittings, brackets and catches could speed reassembly. The ease of transmitting the images can have an added bonus when seeking advice from specialists. They say a picture speaks a thousand words. It also transcends language barriers!

FORWARD PLANNING

Two options are available to the amateur restorer faced with the prospect of removing Traveller wood. One requires more manpower and more storage space. This involves removal of the complete wood frame, including the roof section as one unit. This approach is particularly useful, if retaining the original wood in an undamaged state is a priority. The other method involves the removal of one section at a time. This is more suited to the home restorer, and is therefore the approach which will be described in the pages which follow.

REMOVING THE REAR DOORS

The first task is to remove the rear doors. Occasionally, this can be a straightforward job involving removing both of the inner door stays by undoing the screws holding them to the doors, undoing the nuts on the hinges, and then simply lifting the doors away from the rest of the frame. In all probability the nuts will be rusted into place and the whole bolt will turn. It is now rare to find a Traveller which has not had the doors replaced at some time. As a consequence, there is no guarantee that original specification nuts will have been fitted. Newer metric nuts are often used, so you could be using anything from a ¼in AF to an 11mm spanner. There is little point in trying to save the bolts, so it is easier and quicker to

---

GLOSSARY

Boot well: Rear floor panel behind the petrol tank and below the rear base rails.
B-post: The pillars directly behind the front doors.
Cant rail: Wood rail immediately below the roof, connecting the front and rear pillars.
Chamfer: Bevelled edge on the corner of a piece of wood, i.e. the rear door centre rail, allowing the water to run off.
Drift: Also known as a drift punch used to shape or align two surfaces, i.e. aluminium corners of the roof guttering.
Fillet: A wood strip for holding the metal panels or glass in place. On the Traveller, wood fillets are also used as in-fills in the window runners and the cant rails, and a metal fillet is fixed to the waist rail capping.
Former: A pattern used to shape or fix a panel to.
Forstner bit: A hole-cutting drill bit with multiple cutting faces for making an accurate and clean hole in wood.
Hardura: Traditional boot material for classic cars, consisting of jute felt backing with a wipe-clean vinyl surface.
Inch: Abbreviated as 'in' below, with metric equivalents given as well.
Rebate or rabbet: A woodworking term for a grove cut in the surface.
Sash clamps: Adjustable long straight clamps, used for holding work together while glue dries.
Scotchbrite: Proprietary brand of abrasive similar to a kitchen scourer which is used to give a key to painted surfaces.
Tenon: Tongue forming part of a woodworking joint, as in a mortice and tenon, or a housing joint.
Waist rail: Section of wood running immediately below the rear side windows of a Traveller.
Additional note: Reference to screw sizes are made as follows:
Imperial or metric size plus the generally accepted number of the screw. For example, ¾in number 6 or 1in number 8 refers to the length followed by the gauge. 5mm x 25mm is the gauge followed by the length.

Dealing with seized bolts the easy way.

GLASS REMOVAL

Before attempting to remove the rear side windows, various internal wood cappings and other fittings will need to be unscrewed and removed. The fixings for the rear door stays and the support brackets for the rear seats should be removed prior to undoing the five Phillips headed screws which secure the inner waist (middle) rail. With the screws removed, it should be possible to prise the capping away from the waist rail. A flat screw driver or old chisel placed underneath should break the seal and allow the capping to be removed. Attention should now turn to the cant (top) rail capping and the front pillar cappings. With the screws removed, these should come away quite easily. In the case of the front pillar capping, the upper seat belt fixings will need to be removed first.

grind the nuts off.

A super-fine cutting disc will enable this to be done without damaging the hinges. The lower hinge bolts should then be knocked through the pillar and the inner metal bracket. The remains of the upper bolts can be left in place, unless they are still in good condition and are the original bolts with a hooked head to stop them turning. Once the hinges have been removed from the pillars and the doors, they should be carefully put to one side. A note should be made of which hinge is which, as they are handed, and there are differences between the top and bottom hinges. Before they are re-fitted it is advisable to strip them down, spray the cast iron body, and then replace the internal parts.

> **FOREMAN'S TIP**
> Before trying to remove old screws, place the correct screwdriver head securely in place and tap firmly once or twice with a hammer.

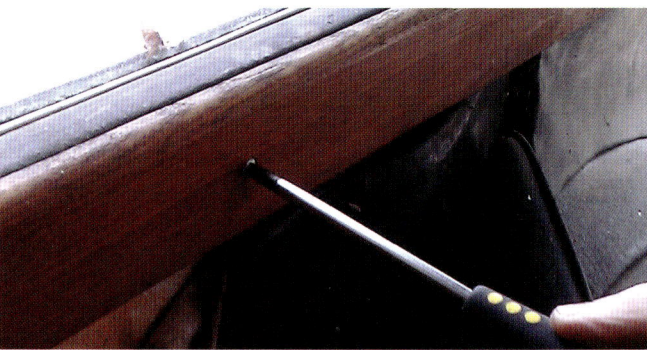

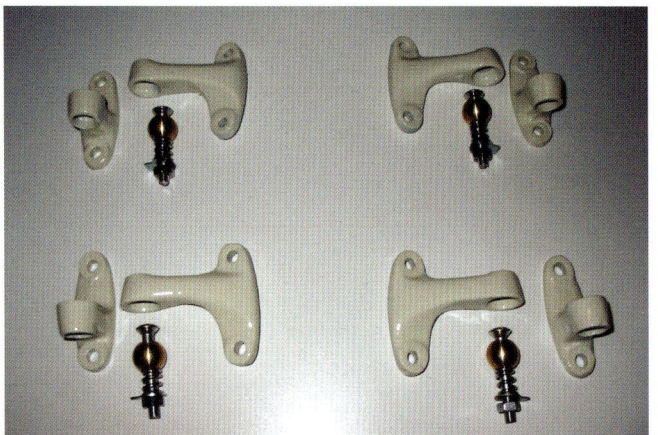

Hinge repair kits ready to fit.

Removing waist rail cappings.

WOODWORK – DISMANTLING

With the middle rail cappings removed, the vinyl side panels can now be lifted out. This will expose the inside of the aluminium panels and the window runners. At this stage it is advisable to remove the black cover for the petrol filler pipe, which is secured by a few self-tapping screws.

Removing petrol pipe cover.

The side of the window runners, which in all probability will be a mixture of rusty metal and moss covered felt, will now be visible. Removal of the glass will require it to be lifted out with the runners attached. Before attempting this, unscrew the middle window lock latch and then, starting at the front end of the rear window, slide a flat old chisel under the runner and gently lift the runner and glass and pull towards the inside of the car. This operation may need to be repeated along the length of the rear window until it is free.

Remove and retain window securing bracket.

Remaining interior cappings being removed, allowing the windows to be taken out.

Screws through wheel arch flange. Hopefully a screwdriver will work but it is more likely that a grinder will be needed.

chisel placed alongside the screw head, a sharp firm hit with hammer should see the screw head taken clean off. A grinder can be used on the more exposed screws, provided care is exercised. However there are places where the grinder can't be used, including the three screws located below the boot floor. Usually a chisel can be slid between the floor and side panel for the top two. If the lower of the three does not unscrew, then the head will need to be drilled off.

REMOVING BUMPERS AND LIGHT FITTINGS

The rear bumper is secured by two nuts (usually $^{11}/_{16}$in W or $^{13}/_{16}$in AF) which are rarely a problem to remove. Some may need a little encouragement with a liberal application of WD 40, if they haven't been removed for a while. The wiring from the number plate lights will need to be detached from the rear loom. With the wiring disconnected the bumper assembly can be lifted off as a complete unit.

Removing windows and old window runners.

> **FOREMAN'S TIP**
> Care should be taken not to accidentally place the glass on a concrete floor, corner first, as it will shatter explosively.

The glass will then lift out. The old window runner should be disposed of. This operation should then be repeated with the front window. The glass should be stored carefully, to prevent it being damaged before re-installation.

With the windows removed, there will be better access to the inside of the frames. Clearly visible now will be a line of round-headed screws which follow the shape of the wheel arch and hold the frame to the inner wheel arch flange.

These screws will need to be removed. If luck is on your side, they may come out using the screwdriver and hammer technique described earlier. The more likely outcome is that most of the screws will be rusted in place, and because they only have a small head, they will quickly round off. There are many time-consuming ways of dealing with this problem, but experience has shown that the quickest results can be achieved using an old chisel and lump hammer. With the

Bumper nuts are often rusted solid.

WOODWORK – DISMANTLING

Bumper off.

Typical mess of rear light wiring.

holders. It is useful at this stage to make a note of which wires go where, in order to save searching through the wiring diagram when it comes to reassembly. Usually the indicator wires are longer than the rear and brake lights, so these don't need marking. It is useful to note which of the connectors the red (rear light) wire goes to by simply putting a red mark on the bulb holder. The black wires (earth) go to the connector closest to the bulb, and the positives to the connectors on the end of the sprung part. With the red wire marked, then the position of the others can easily be worked out. It is highly likely that some of the holders and all of the rubber boots will need replacing, but at this stage they should be retained for future reference. The reflector is held on by one screw which will be clearly visible, once the bezel and lens have been removed.

The rear light lenses can be easily removed, once the chrome bezels have been prised out of the rubber boots. This is best done using a flat head screwdriver. The bulb holders are held in place with three screws.

Once removed, the wires can be unplugged from their

Lights out

87

REMOVING THE HEADLINING

Before getting on with removing the wood, it is sensible to get the headlining out of the way. With the cant rail cappings already removed, the edge of the headlining will be visible.

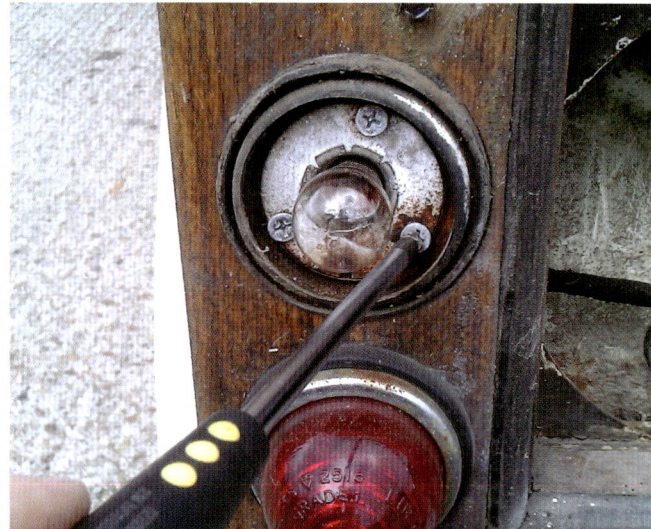

Staples or tacks holding headlining.

Remove screws holding rear headlining capping.

Remove, and usually discard, original light fittings and rubbers.

Remove rear pillar corner bracket.

WOODWORK – DISMANTLING

The rear of the headlining is held in place by five screws through a material covered ply former. Begin by removing these screws. If original, the sides of the headlining will be held in place with small black tacks. If it is a replacement headlining, staples may have been used. Either way these need to be carefully removed. The back of the headlining with the ply former attached will drop down, and the tacks holding the material to the inner roof rails will become visible. Remove these from the rear of the roof rails, then repeat with the front rail.

replace the headlining, particularly if it is going to be reused. At some point the tacks holding the front section of the headlining will need to be removed, to expose the bolt heads holding the roof in place. At this stage they are best left in place.

Two sockets or spanners required to remove cab roof bolts.

With the headlining out of the way, the top rear pillar corner brackets will be exposed. These should be removed.

At the front there are also some top corner brackets. These should be left in place as they are screwed into the cant rail. Once they become accessible, they should be removed and discarded. These brackets serve no useful purpose, unless the complete wood frame is being assembled off the car, as it would have been at the factory.

Rear pillar top corner brackets removed.

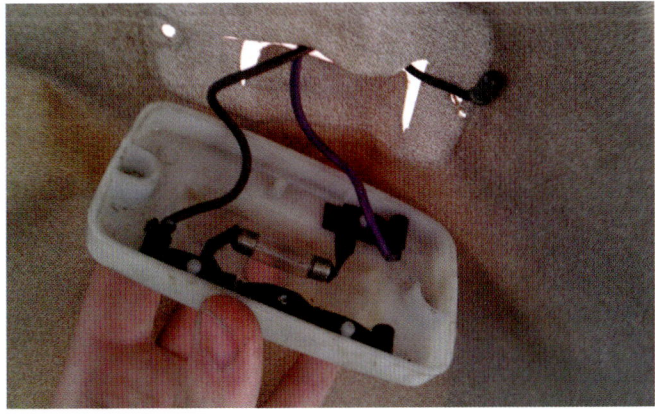

Detach interior light. Beware permanently live purple wire.

The interior light will need to be unscrewed and the wires disconnected. It is advisable to tape up the end of the purple wire (live). By this stage the headlining will only be held at the front. With the few screws holding the material covered capping undone, along with a few tacks along the front top rail, the headlining can be rolled up and removed from the car. Alternatively, the lining can be left attached to the two inner roof rails and left in place until the sides are off. Using this method, the headlining can be rolled up complete with inner roof rails still tacked on. This can make it easier to

> **FOREMAN'S TIP**
> Over the years, the rear door stay mechanism will wear and no longer hold the door open. Unless a non-original, but effective, telescopic door stay is purchased, or a good second-hand replacement can be found, refurbishment of the original will be needed. This is best attempted after removing the arm from the fixing on the middle capping rail. The stay has a slope on the underside. Over time this will have become rounded off. To rectify the problem it will need reshaping. This is best done using a hand file to square off as shown. Using a grinder is quicker but it is easy to overdo it. If this happens, then the door will not shut at all or attempting to close it will be so difficult that it will put a strain on the hinges. Modifications seen over the years include small holes drilled through the stay and a peg on a chain fitted. Once the door is open, the peg is put in place through the hole and the door is secured. This method works well, but it is important not to forget that the peg is in place. Failure to do so will put unnecessary strain on the hinges, and the joints in the door will be put at risk.

PREPARATION FOR REMOVING THE WOOD FRAMES

The side frames are a structural assembly, bolted and screwed to the car body, and then capped off by an aluminium roof nailed to the top rails. The first job is to remove the roof guttering which starts life as an open C section which, after it has been tacked to the roof, then has the top section of the C folded down over the tack heads. It has been suggested in previous manuals that the top section can be lifted up, the original gutter removed and then re-used. It is not possible to do this and achieve a satisfactory finish. Once aluminium has been stretched, it will not go back into shape, and trying to make good any dents or ripples will not be effective. Fitting the guttering is almost the final job after fitting the wood and the quality of finish of the whole job can be ruined by a badly fitted drip moulding. So the best option is to fit new. However, the standard of finish will be decided very much by how the old gutter is removed. It is imperative that the roof remains totally flat.

REMOVING THE ROOF GUTTERING

Tools required: Mole grips, wide chisel, hand held grinder with cutting disc and sanding disc.

Start at the front on each side by the cab T-rubber. First gently tap a wide chisel (at least 1in or 25mm wide) down between the guttering and roof panel, being careful not to dent or ripple the roof at all. With the guttering slightly away from the roof, it is possible to get a grip with some mole grips. With the mole grips tight, start pulling away from the roof and towards the rear of the car. The gutter is held by tacks about every 4in (100mm). The old tack heads will pull through the gutter relatively easily, but it is important not to lever the mole grips against the roof. Once enough guttering has been pulled away (normally 1 or 2ft, 300 to 600mm) it should be possible to release the mole grips and continue the task by hand, bending the guttering up and down, and then back, until it pulls away from the next tack head. Continue

down the car and round the corner until the whole piece has been removed. Repeat for the other side. The exposed tack heads which have been pulled through the guttering will now need to be removed. Avoid using pincers or side cutters to remove them, as this will leave a row of dents. Instead use a grinder with a thin cutting disc to take the heads off. The roof will then be held by just a few tacks which have been countersunk into the aluminium.

Protecting the roof is the most important thing. Two options are available. Either use a flat, old, but sharp chisel, or a grinder with an ultra thin cutting disc. If saving the wood which is being removed is a priority, using a sharp chisel is the best option. Place the underside of the chisel against the wood with the blade ready to slide under the roof. Stand to one side and give the chisel a sharp firm tap to break the tack head off in one hit. Any damage to the wood will only be superficial. Alternatively, if the wood is being discarded, then run the cutting disc of the grinder under the roof until the tack has been cut. There will be a lot of smoke, and a smell of burning wood, but damage to the roof will be avoided.

Carefully prise away guttering.

WOODWORK – DISMANTLING

The final job before lifting the roof away is to sand the edge of the roof flat while it is still supported by the wood. Old paint, sealant, and filler will have created a lumpy line where the gutter fits. By sanding back around 20-30mm (say 1in) of the edge of the roof using an orbital sander, or by putting a sanding disc on the grinder, a perfect flat surface can be achieved on to which the new guttering can be attached. The reason for doing this now is that once the roof has been re-fitted, it will be on new and freshly finished wood, and it is important to minimise the risk of any damage being caused. It is also vital to note that if the roof is not going to be re-sprayed and only the new guttering is to be painted, then any sanding should be confined to the area that will be covered by the new drip moulding.

Removing tack heads without damaging the roof.

With everything ready, the roof will now pull away from the wood. At this stage just lift it a couple of centimetres (say 1in) to free it off. Careful use of a wide chisel will help pop it off the old cut tacks. While it is still bolted to the front cab, roof movement will be limited.

REMOVING THE SIDES

If the wood is to be discarded, the job of removing the sides is relatively straightforward now that the preparation work has been completed. Begin by removing the section of window runner sitting in the rebate at the top of the rear pillar and then using a sharp saw, cut through the top of the pillar just under the roof. Follow this by cutting through again just above the waist rail, and remove the section of the rear pillar. This will allow the rear top rail, which is still attached to the cant rails, to be pulled down about 50cm (say 20in). This will expose the screws holding the inner roof rails to the cant rails. If possible remove the screws. In the event that they will not move, cut the cant rail either side of the roof rails. The remaining piece of wood will then unscrew. Before cutting through the cant rail, remove the window runner, cant rail fillets, and both the rubber buffers from each side. The rubber buffers should be screwed into the cant rail at the extreme rear of the outer window runner, and at the end of the cant rail fillet. Save these items as they are not available new. With the roof rails removed, the remains of the cant rails can be pulled right down to expose the front top corner brackets. If possible, remove the two screws into the cant rail (this usually means chiselling between the bracket and cant rail as there isn't much space for a screwdriver) and break the cant rails away from the car.

Inner roof rail meets cant rail.

As the screws from around the wheel arch flange have already been removed, the only fixings left to undo are the lower rear pillar bolt, the rear pillar screws, and the front pillar bolts. It is also worth checking to see if a splash plate has been welded to the car under the foot rail. Normally the splash plate will be a separate plate screwed to the foot rail, and will come away with the frame. Sometimes a splash plate will have been welded to the underside of the car at a later date; if this is so then any screws through the splash plate will also need to be removed.

The rear pillar bolts can be a bit of a problem. The nut on the coach bolt will be visible inside the rear corner bracket. It is likely to be rusty, buried in general debris, and seized to the bolt. If this is the case, and it normally is, then the bottom of the rear pillar can easily be split away with a chisel and mallet. The bolt can be ground off after the wood is removed. The rear pillar corner brackets, which also support the load bay floor, are held to the inside face of the rear pillars by two round-head screws. Note the black ply packing pieces sandwiched between these brackets and pillars. It is important when reassembling that these are replaced. The two screws are located just above and just below the load bay floor, and the lower one especially will probably need to be removed with a grinder or chisel.

If the frames are original, there will be pair of screws through the inside face of the base rail tenons into the back of the rear pillar. This will only be the case if the frames are original. It is unlikely that replacement wood will have had the screws fitted. It is impossible to get to these screws, so it will be a matter of splitting away the bottom of the rear pillar with a mallet and chisel. If this has had to be done to free the main rear pillar bolts, then the chances are that enough has been broken away to access these screws.

Breaking wood away from seized rear pillar bolts.

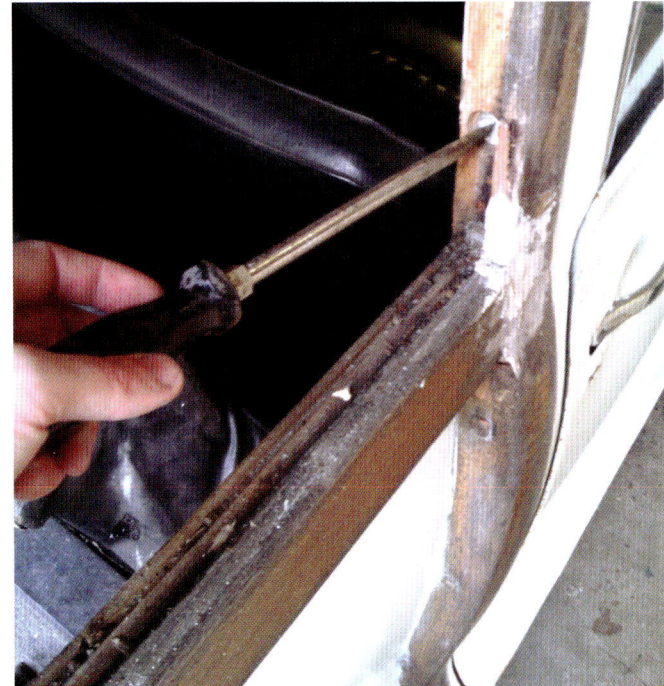

With the rear pillars free, the wheel arch flanges unscrewed, and any foot rail screws removed, all that remains is to undo the front pillar bolts. These could well have been in place for upwards of forty years, but a firm tap with a hammer or the use of a handy impact driver should see them unscrew. If they really are stubborn, then mole grips should get the job done. Occasionally, if the bolts have

Phillips number 3 screwdriver for the front pillar bolts.

WOODWORK – DISMANTLING

Stubborn bolts sometimes need mole grips.

side aluminium panel, complete with filler cap. It is then advisable to re-fit it in the inside of the car to seal the tank and reduce the risk of a spark getting into the tank and causing an explosion.

started to rust, the captive nuts hidden inside the B-posts will break free, and the bolt will just spin round. If this is the case, and as time goes on this tends to happen more often, then to get the wood free it will be necessary to chisel the wood away from around the bolt. A sharp chisel and a mallet is all that is required. Split the wood down the grain and it will come away fairly easily. Coping with the spinning bolt is more of a problem. Choices include either cutting a slot into the inside face of the B post and grinding off and replacing the captive nut or welding a metal plate over the hole, then drilling and re-tapping ($5/16$in BSF).

Before the left hand side can be removed, the petrol filler pipe needs to be taken out. This is easily done by loosening the screw on the clamp which holds the rubber pipe to the metal filler pipe. This will then pull through the hole on the

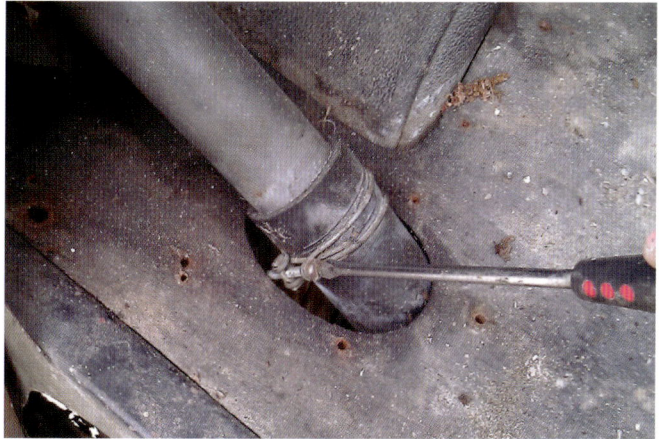

Petrol filler pipe out and made safe.

You can now attempt to lift the sides away from the car. This may not prove to be an easy task, as the sealant around the flange panel may still be holding the wood in place. A large flat screwdriver should be enough to break the seal and lever the side away complete with wing and panels attached. The roof, as it is still bolted to the cab, can be left *in situ*, but should be supported if the vehicle is moved.

> **TIME SAVING OPTIONS**
>
> If the cab roof is not going to be re-sprayed and the T-rubber is still in good condition, there is no need to remove the roof from the car. This will save a lot of time. However, if there is any doubt about the condition of the T-rubber, it is best not to take the risk of leaving the old one in place.

MORRIS MINOR TRAVELLER – THE COMPLETE COMPANION

Accessing coach bolt retaining base rails.

The last section of wood to be removed is the base rail assembly, which is covered by a metal rear valance. Both of these items are held in place by two coach bolts into the metal corner bracket, and four bolts which pass through the boot well floor. The nuts on the coach bolts should unscrew without a problem, and even if the bolts will not come out easily, the base rails can easily be levered away from the corner brackets. The four bolts through the bottom of the base rails can be removed either with a spanner, or by grinding the bolt heads off. If the base rails have previously been changed, the bolts may have been replaced with screws and washers. This type of fitting has the advantage of reducing the risk of rot in the bottom base rails.

MOMENT OF TRUTH

With all the wood finally removed, the extent of the work ahead will finally be revealed. The typical Traveller restoration will normally involve some rectification work, to the boot well floor and wheel arch flange panels. The positive news is that everything is easy to work on and very accessible. No matter how bad the metalwork is, repair panels are available, and fitting them is within the scope of any competent welder. The technique and skills required for welding is beyond the remit of this book, but the importance of aligning any replacement panels accurately cannot be stressed enough. In particular, it is vital not to undertake a final fit of the wheel arch flange panels, without having the newly assembled sides available to offer up to the car. Care taken here will pay dividends later on.

The preparation of the exposed metal work is very important, regardless of whether welding is required. This is a unique opportunity to protect all the areas that hopefully will not be seen for at least another thirty years. All the exposed metal needs rust treating and protecting. The 'to do' list includes filling the box sections with Waxoyl or an equivalent rust inhibitor, and depending on the extent of the restoration, undercoating and painting the inner wings and the boot well floor.

Sides removed.

WOODWORK – DISMANTLING

PICTORIAL GUIDE TO ESSENTIAL STRUCTURAL REPAIRS

The Traveller shown illustrates the typical problems which can be encountered, once the woodwork has been removed. It is by no means the worst that may be encountered, but rectification work is required. The boot well floor is showing signs of delaminating, and the wheel arch panels are in need of repair. The rear corner brackets are rusted through and will need to be replaced.

Before cutting any of the metalwork prior to repair, the rear load bay floor will need to be removed. The ply panels are held by a series of 2ba machine screws into the metal frame, and by wood screws along the front edge. Once removed, these panels will lift away from the metal frame quite easily. The metal frame is held in position by two bolts into captive nuts in each corner, and two screws at the front. With these removed the metal frame can be taken out, which will free up access to all the areas that may need to be worked on.

New corner brackets can be welded on, if necessary, and the whole thing painted in a black gloss. The inner rear corner brackets are welded to the inner wing, and if they need replacing, they will need to be cut out after first unbolting the bumper iron (¼inW spanner). The bumper irons can then be removed, by either unbolting from the rear floor, or twisting to the centre of the car out of the way.

This is typical of what will be uncovered once the wood has been removed.

Cut away all the rusty panels.

Fit new wheel arch flanges, bootwell floor and boxing plate extensions.

WOODWORK – DISMANTLING

New wheel arch flanges, bootwell floor and boxing plate extensions fitted and ready to paint.

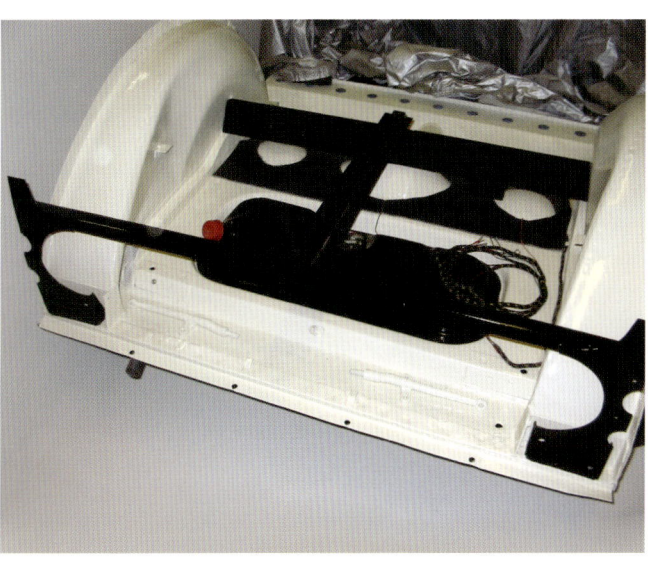

Painted, new corner brackets fitted and ready for the wood frames.

CHAPTER 9
WOODWORK – PREPARING AND FINISHING

A typical complete wood kit.

A selection of recommended finishes.

A replacement wood kit should contain all the parts required to replace the wood frames. The frames come assembled, unless a flat-pack export kit has been ordered. All fixings and trim fittings such as new window runners, roof guttering, and all fillets are included.

The wood frames come as bare unfinished wood which means that before they are fitted, a considerable amount of effort must be devoted to preparing, preserving, and applying a suitable wood finish. Time and effort spent at this stage will pay dividends later. As well as adding years to the life of the wood, it will make subsequent maintenance tasks a lot easier.

WHICH FINISH?

If you were to ask a hundred people the best way to protect the wood on a Traveller, you would probably get a hundred different answers. The problem is that most of them would be at least partially right. Numerous factors need to be taken into account when considering the most effective type of finish to apply. Considerations include how the vehicle is being used and cared for, where in the world the owner lives, and whether the vehicle is garaged at night. Then there is the not inconsiderable matter of personal choice in the selection of finish. Should it be light coloured, have a gloss or matt finish, or be capable of withstanding extremes of temperature and humidity? With so many variables to contend with, it is difficult to come up with a 'one-fits-all' solution. The text which follows provides some answers and recommendations, based on thirty years of experience in such matters.

ASH BUILT FRAMES

Ash has been used in the manufacture of vehicles ever since carriages took to the roads. It has many fine qualities, not least of which are that is light, very strong, flexible, and stable. It very rarely splits or twists due to variations of humidity or temperature. It is attractive when varnished, and for a hard wood it is relatively easy to work. It does, however, have one major drawback. It has a tendency to rot when it is allowed to get wet and remain wet. Ash is a very dry wood with no natural resins or oils. Unlike teak with its oil, pitch pine with its resin, and oak with its tannins, ash needs assistance to withstand the elements. Without treatment, ultra-violet light will break up the surface, damp will be easily absorbed, and fungi spores will soon get a hold and quickly eat through the structure of the wood. With no finish at all the wood will get wet, show signs of surface splitting, and very quickly go grey and become discoloured. It will however be slow to develop rot, unless damp is trapped in the wood. If this happens, it will begin to rot very quickly.

A wood frame which has been sealed will be fine for a while, but after the summer sun has dried the wood, hairline cracks will begin to appear at the joints. Once the wet season starts, water will inevitably get in through these cracks. When the rain stops, the only way for the water to get out is through the same small cracks. This is unlikely to happen and, where the water has been retained, a black area will gradually appear on the surface of the wood and will spread behind the finish. If left untreated, this will develop into wet rot. As the frame on the Morris Minor Traveller is structural, and subject to inspection for MOT Test purposes, failure to cope with this problem could eventually lead to MOT failure.

No matter how much time is spent on coating the surface, or how good the product used may be, it is inevitable that eventually this will happen. Even if an epoxy coating with a two-pack polyurethane varnish is used, it will still happen. There are no fit-and-forget finishes when it comes to Traveller wood. It is also an unfortunate fact that the more durable the finish applied, the more difficult it will be to

WOODWORK – PREPARING AND FINISHING

remove, and the greater the potential for causing damage to the surface of the wood. This will also happen with the various oils on the market which harden like a varnish, but do not have the same durability. It applies to the saturation finishes, which also set like a varnish slightly under the surface. This makes their removal even more difficult. All this may give the impression that having a varnish-type finish is not the way to go, but this is not the case. Having an original type finish with a high gloss is still possible. However, being aware of the inherent problems associated with different types of finish allows for informed choices to be made and other options considered.

TYPES OF FINISH

If your Traveller is kept permanently outdoors and exposed to the elements, it is advisable that a fully sealed finish such as varnish or a hard setting oil is not used. Oils which set to a hard finish act like a weak varnish and are better suited to fine finishes on interior furniture. This applies to such products as the standard Danish oil, and although there are superior versions, with an ultra violet screen, they are not very successful on ash unless your Traveller is garaged. There are some non-setting natural oils which work well but they will need topping up regularly, will stay semi-wet, and attract a lot of dirt and dust. They are designed for topping up the natural oils in teak, mahogany, and similar woods.

For a Traveller that is not garaged, the only practical solution is to select a micro porous wood finish which will let the wood breathe. It is a matter of accepting that the wood will get wet and a case of letting it dry out. Micro porous finishes have improved dramatically over the years. One of the drawbacks in the past was the dark colouring of the micro porous wood stains, which tended to increase as more coats were added. With the Sikkens Cetol system, it is now possible to get a satin finish in a natural, but not clear, ash finish. A welcome added bonus is that it is both easy to apply and maintain.

To summarise, in simple terms there are two types of finish which are of practical and aesthetic use on ash. These are high-gloss fully sealed or semi-opaque satin micro porous. There are many different products on the market but the ones mentioned in the text are those which have been found to provide the most versatile, durable, and practical finishes.

STAGE 1: PRESERVING THE WOOD

The first and very important task is to preserve and basecoat the wood. Most typical clear wood preservatives will offer protection against infestation from beetles, worms, and fungi spores. They will not give protection from UV under the surface of the wood where it is needed. They also have the disadvantage of highlighting the natural differences in the colour of the wood from one section to another. This becomes even more pronounced if only one or two sections are being fitted.

After many years of experimentation, the Woodies' favoured option for the perfect preservative basecoat is a mix of Sikkens Cetol HLS in the colour of choice (see photo of samples and descriptions) and Cuprinol clear preservative or an equivalent product. The recommended mix is approximately 50/50, allowing for some variation depending on the colour required. It is important to remember that the colour when first applied will be considerably darker than when it dries. The equal mix gives the same honey tone of the original factory finish. The advantage of using Cuprinol in the mix is that it takes the Sikkens basecoat deeper into the surface of the wood.

This mixture should be applied liberally by using a brush. By standing the frames on a plastic sheet, any excess will be absorbed through the end grain of the front and rear pillars. If two coats are being applied, this is best done 'wet on wet' to ensure the benefits of full absorption. At this stage any thoughts on the quality of finish is secondary to applying as much preservative as possible. Allow to dry for up to one hour, before wiping all the excess off with a clean dry rag, on all the areas which will be visible once the frames are on the car. White spirit may be needed on the cloth, if this task is left for more than an hour. This will leave a silky, waxy finish, free from streaks and runs.

A PROBLEM AREA – AND THE SOLUTION

There are many schools of thought about how to protect the drain holes in the middle rail. They are seen as a problem area, but they don't need to be. In the production era, many Travellers had brass or plastic tubes fitted in the drain holes. Instead of helping drainage, the tubes themselves became a trap for moisture and, in almost every case, the area around these tubes began to rot. The reason for this was that as soon as a new material was introduced next to the wood, damp was generated between the two surfaces, with no way of drying it out. The wood around the drain holes tends to rot, because once they become blocked, water accumulates, and there is nowhere for it to go.

The best way of overcoming this problem is to apply only basecoat and preservative to the drain holes. Block them from underneath, fill them up and leave overnight. Do this during the base coating stage, and repeat the process over the three days while the frames are drying. When the frames are ready to fit, let the excess run out. It is important not to varnish or seal the drain holes. For further advice about on-going preservation techniques and ways to extend the life of the waist rails, refer to the maintenance section below.

STAGE 2: EXTERIOR FINISH

1) **High Gloss Traditional Finish**

If a gloss finish is required, then there are a number of

IMPORTANT
You must make sure that the preservative used is solvent based.

FOREMAN'S TIP
If the weather is hot and sunny, apply the basecoats and the top coat in the shade to prevent them drying too quickly. Leave to dry for three days. If no Cuprinol or an equivalent product has been used, then reduce to one day.

Applying the basecoat preservative

FOREMAN'S TIP

If a tried and tested combination is required for an exterior gloss finish, Blackfriars Exterior Gloss plus 10 per cent Owatrol oil is the Woodies' preferred choice. Apply three or four coats, leaving twenty-four hours between coats. If care is exercised when applying each coat, it should only be necessary to sand down the finish before applying the last coat. A Scotchbrite pad or 320 grit sandpaper should suffice. The results should be excellent, providing a superb gloss finish, which will be flexible and will not crack or peel.

options. It is best to avoid cheap yacht varnish finishes, which are brittle and have a tendency to peel. Also avoid polyurethane finishes. It is best to select a good varnish which is flexible and has an ultra-violet screen. At the top of the price range there are proven marine quality varnishes such as Epiphanes, but Blackfriars Exterior Gloss is a readily available high quality product which, when mixed with 10 per cent Owatrol oil, creates the perfect product for a high quality finish, ideally suited for use on the Morris Minor Traveller. Owatrol oil is a paint conditioner which gives a brush stroke free finish and added flexibility. It can be added to any paint or varnish, and has the advantage of being a rust inhibitor. Any surplus can be used on the exposed metalwork before the frames are fitted. It is well worth the minimal cost involved in buying a small tin.

2) Micro Porous Exterior Wood Stain

If circumstances determine that a micro porous exterior wood stain finish is the best option for the long term welfare of a particular Traveller, then first apply by using the same basecoat and Cuprinol mixture as for the gloss top coat. The application of three coats of Sikkens Cetol filter 7, in the colour selected, will suffice to provide adequate protection. Though other brands are available, Sikkens has a more natural translucent finish to it. The Classic range allows for an extensive range of colours to be mixed. A very natural and attractive ash finish can be achieved.

VERY IMPORTANT

If the micro porous finish is selected, then some additional work will be a priority. All the inside surfaces of the wood will need to be fully sealed with a varnish, or even a gloss paint. All areas which are hidden when fitted need to be impervious to moisture. That way all the water that gets into the frame from the outside surfaces will also dry through the micro porous finish. If, after a very bad winter, there is still darkening at the joints, even when fully dry, it is easy to lightly sand back and add another coat. Be assured that the whole finish will not need to be removed. This is a great advantage, if the Traveller has to remain outside in all weathers.

MAINTENANCE

Whichever finish is selected and no matter how diligently the finish has been applied, there is only one way to ensure that the wood lasts and looks good for many years: regular maintenance. Anyone fortunate enough to own a wooden boat would not consider going into a new season, without adding a coat of paint or varnish. A Traveller owner should be no different except, instead of applying a fresh protective coat in the spring, it should be applied in order to protect the car for the winter. The best time in the UK for maintenance is in late August or early September. The heat of the sun will have done its worst and even though the wood still looks good, there will be hairline cracks at the joints. A light rub down with fine sandpaper, Scotchbrite, or kitchen scourer and white spirit, will give enough of a key to apply a fresh top coat of the chosen exterior finish. Spending two hours once a year doing this will pay dividends. However if it is left for another year, there is always the risk of having to undertake a complete strip back. For Travellers which are permanently garaged and only taken out for shows or on sunny days, then a different time frame will apply. In these circumstances, probably every three or four years should suffice.

As well as applying a fresh top coat, it is beneficial to protect the wood under the window runners. This is an area that tends to be ignored year on year. However, it is a part of the frame where damp accumulates and remains. The window runners hold moisture and are the perfect breeding ground for fungi spores. Taking the windows out is not something many people will want to do very frequently, so a useful alternative is to tape up the drain holes in the waist rail, having first checked that they are not blocked. Having done this then pour about 1/3 litre (a bit more than half a pint) of clear wood preservative along the runners. This will run into the drain holes, and everywhere else water will get to! It will also kill any unwelcome infestations. If left to soak in overnight, the preservative will soak into the end grain in the drain holes. However, care needs to be exercised, as any preservative that runs onto the paintwork will need to be wiped off immediately, so as to avoid it staining the paintwork.

CHAPTER 10
WOODWORK – FITTING THE FRAME

After all the endless hours of removing the old frames, preparing the chassis, and protecting and finishing the wood, it will be a relief to finally begin the process of re-assembling the Traveller. However, it is important to resist the temptation to rush to fit the frames straight away. Strange as it may seem, it is best to do as much work on the frames off the car as possible. When the sides eventually go on to the car, the panels, wings, and upper window runners will need to have been fitted. It is much easier to fit a rear wing with the side upside down in a Workmate, rather than lying under the car trying to line up the wing, hold it in place, and get the screws in at the right angle. This task is made even more difficult by the fact that new metal rear wings are not always the same shape or the best of fits.

Before fitting the panels, it is a good idea to fit the top window runners. It is quicker and easier to complete this task with the frame upside down. Begin by tacking the small rubber buffer to the rear end of the cant rail before trimming and fitting the full-length outer window runner. Allow sufficient space, about 5mm (3/16in), for the front pillar capping to slot in. The runner is held in place by ¾in number 6 screws. Next fit the wood fillet which runs from the front of the cant rail to about a third of the way along. Screw the small rubber block in place and then fit the window runner into the remaining space which should be about 75cm (30in) long.

FITTING ALUMINIUM SIDE PANELS

It is advisable to place the complete side on to an old blanket on a workbench or table before attempting to fit the aluminium side panels. Fitting these is fairly straightforward, but it is important that the panels sit flat, to avoid creating ripples in the soft alloy while fixing them in position.

Put a thin bead of black caulking sealant on the edge of the wood where the panel is to be fitted. Carefully position the panel and then, using a flat piece of wood and some G clamps, press it into place. The leading edge of the front panel will need a former, with a curve, which follows the shape of the front pillar. Once the panel is flat to the wood and the sealant has been compressed evenly to about 3mm (1/8in), then the ¾in number 6 screws can be put in place. Do not over tighten. A power screwdriver with a torque setting is

Fitting the aluminium panels. Take time to make sure there are no ripples.

panel goes into the rear pillar. This will need to be wedged into place, in order to force the panel flat to the rebate. The bottom of the foot rail is also held in place by a short wood fillet. Once both panels are firmly and evenly attached, turn the side over and trim off any excess caulking sealant, and clean the edge of the panels with white spirit.

FITTING THE REAR WING

A more difficult task to get right is the fitting of the rear wing. Before attaching the wing, wing piping needs to be fitted to the wheel arch. This needs to be positioned carefully before being stapled into place. However, care needs to be taken not to get too close to the edge of the wood.

Carefully cut the wing piping around the foot rail contour.

The wing piping used around the front of the wheel arch will need cutting to get a good fit. From there it is a matter of working from the front to the back. The piping needs to fit snugly against the edge of the wood, and any gaps need to be dealt with at this stage. Once the wing is on, it will be too late to rectify any areas of badly fitting piping.

For the fitting of the wing screws and washers, a power screwdriver, and a flat screwdriver or chisel will be needed. Originally the rear wings were fixed in position using bolts, which fitted into threaded sleeves set into the wheel arch. In retrospect this was not the best design, as it meant that there

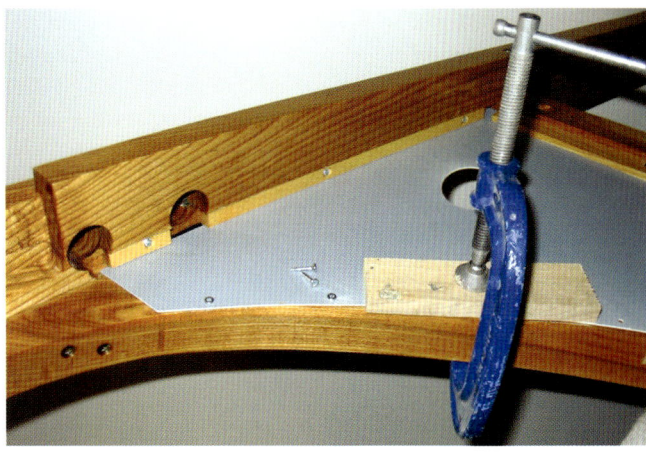

Clamping the panels to the sides to prevent ripple

ideal for this task. The top of the panels along the waist rail are held in place by the middle rail fillet which helps to keep the panels totally flat; 1in number 8 screws will be required to secure this. A wood fillet is also supplied for use where the

WOODWORK – FITTING THE FRAME

was too much metal in a relatively thin section of wood. Inevitably, black staining eventually appeared around these fixings. It is better to fix the wings in position by using about eight 1in number 10 round-headed screws with washers. Alternatively, similar sized, hexagonal headed, self-cutting screws with washers, specifically designed for fixing metal to wood, will give a more original looking finish.

Fit and re-fit the rear wings until they line up correctly.

Rest the wing approximately in place and line up the front edge with the profile of the foot rail. Using a power screwdriver, put the first screw in. If good quality screws are used, the power screwdriver will self-tap the screw into place, and pull the wing in. If in doubt drill a small pilot hole. Work around the wing from front to back, making sure the outside of the wing neatly sits under the wing piping. Insert a screw about every 8in (200mm), or where necessary, to pull the wing tight to the wheel arch. Be careful not to put the screws too close to the front edge of the wood, as this is likely to cause it to split. At the centre of the wing, it will be necessary to use a chisel or screwdriver to lever the wing into place.

Patience will be needed here, mainly because the wings are of variable fit and they often need to be manipulated into the ideal position. For instance, if when positioning the rear of the wing it is proving impossible to pull it into place without risk of creasing the metal, then it may be necessary to remove some of the screws and reposition the wing until the perfect fit is achieved. While doing this it is important to keep referring to the front edge of the wing, as a neat fit around the wing piping is vital to obtain a cosmetically perfect finish.

With the panels and the wing in place, it is a good idea to add some further protection to the wood. You can use an aluminium paint, a quality gloss chassis black, or any paint which will withstand the salt and road debris which will be thrown up into the inner wing. Coat the inside and underneath of the wheel arch, the bottom and inner faces of the foot rail, the inside of the front pillar, and the end grain of the underside of the rear pillar. These are all areas which will not be seen again but which run the risk of getting wet.

FITTING THE WOOD FRAMES

How easy it is to line up the frames will be dependent on how much welding has been done to the inner wings and boot well floor. The rear corner brackets may have been replaced, which means there will be no reference points for centralising the wood. With this scenario, it is advisable to start with the base rail set which will be fully assembled and ready to fit. It is worth making a note here that it is easier to fit the socket for the door mechanism, while the base rails are off the car. The metal rear valance needs to be fitted to the base rails. Most good quality valances will have the holes drilled for the bumper irons, and the coach bolts which attach everything to the rear corner bracket. This means that the assembly can be lifted over the bumper irons, and that the bolt holes can be lined up with the holes drilled in the corner brackets. Getting the base rail assembly correctly centralised at this stage is critical to getting the side frames square.

Fit the door mechanism socket before fitting the base rails.

> **FOREMAN'S TIP**
> When fitting the wing, use smaller screws to start with, such as a 1in number 8 countersunk Pozidrive. When satisfied with the fit, replace with the neater, stronger 1in number 10 round-head screws with washers, or the hexagonal headed fixings.

Base rail assembly ready to fit. Note the small tacks holding the valance in place.

Two large coach bolts are used to secure the base rail assembly. The bottom base rail can either be bolted to the boot well floor as per original specification, or four screws and washers can be used. Whichever method is selected, it is best to wait until the sides are fitted before securing, as some movement of the base rails may be required. The rear corner bracket bolts which fit through the floor also need to be loose, so they can slide backwards or forwards as necessary.

A bead of sealant around the wheel arch flange.

Coach bolt securing the rails.

With the base rail assembly correctly positioned, the first of the sides can be fitted. This job is much easier with two people but this is not essential. Begin by putting a bead of caulking sealant down the inside of the B-post and a thicker bead around the upright of the wheel arch flange. Lift the side and align it to where it is to be fitted, concentrating mainly on the front end. If the side has been pre-fitted before applying the finish, the little cut-out at the top of the front pillar should have been made and the bolt holes opened up as necessary.

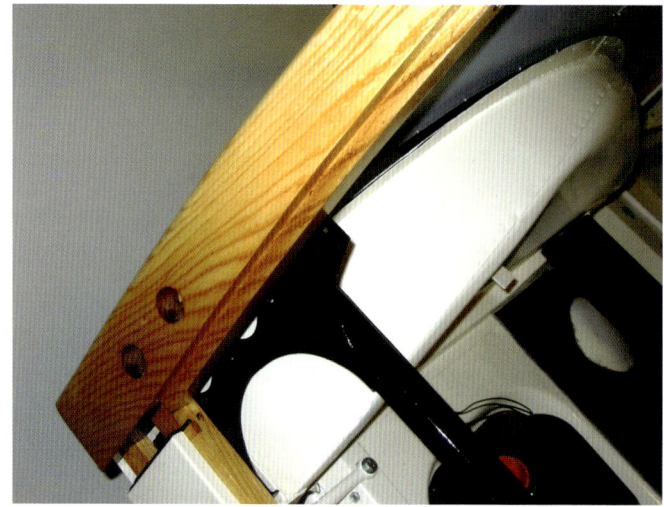

Fit the sides. Pull tight to the base rails.

WOODWORK – FITTING THE FRAME

Hold the side in place and fit the top and middle bolts into the B-post. They need only be hand tight for now. When the alignment of the wood with the B-post is satisfactory, fit the rest of the bolts. At this stage they need only be barely finger tight. With the front secured, move to the rear and pull the rear pillar into place. At this point any number of problems can arise. It is rare that the pillar pulls in easily onto the base rails. Usually the bottom of the rear pillar sits too high or too low, or it is difficult to pull in because part of the wheel arch is fouling the metal flange panel. It is vital at this stage not to put too much stress on the wood frame, as there is a high risk of cracking the wheel arch joints. It is best to gently lift and push the frame into place. Any area around the metal flange that is causing a problem will need to be dressed into place with a hammer. If new flanges have been fitted, using the sides to line them up, then none of these problems should arise. Do not be too concerned that the wood wheel arch does not follow the line of the metal flange. Normally it will be very tight to the lip at the front and drift away towards the rear. The most important consideration is that the inside of the wood seals tightly against the upright flange.

Lining up where to drill the hole for the rear pillar coach bolt can be done as the rear pillars begin to slide on to the tenons of the base rail assembly. This quite easily done by putting a pencil horizontally through the hole in the corner bracket, and marking the distance from the bottom of the rear pillar where the hole needed to be drilled. The distance in from the edge of the pillar is easy to work out.

Put a bead of caulking sealant between the inner face of the pillar and the base rails, and clamp the pillar reasonably tightly into place. Now drill through the rear pillar where marked. Provided the drill is held level, then the hole on the bracket should be easily located. Liberally coat the coach bolts with grease and then push them into place. Once the nut has been fitted and tightened (a little patience and dexterity may be required to get the nut onto the end of the bolt) then finally tighten the bolts holding the corner brackets, fix the base rails to the boot well floor, and tighten the front pillar bolts.

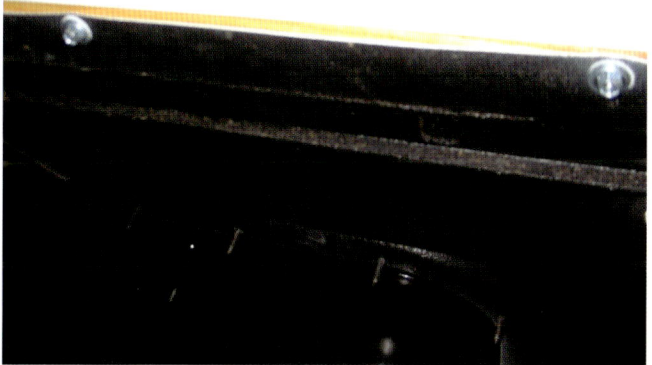

Use Hex head screws to fix the boot well floor to the base rails.

Vital Check
Before putting the screws through the wheel arch flange and fully securing the sides, it is advisable to square up the frame. It is crucial that time is spent now getting everything lined up. An out of square framework cannot be adjusted later.

PREPARING FOR THE REAR DOOR FIT
Fit the newly painted and refurbished hinges to the doors, and then clamp the doors together with a 5mm (3/16in) strip of wood between them. At this stage it is better if the doors are in bare wood and not finished, as final trimming may be needed later. Rest the door assembly onto the base rails, and loosely slot the rear top rail into place. Square up the rear pillars as necessary, by either pushing or pulling until an even gap of between 5 and 8mm (3/16 to 5/16in) all round is achieved. This applies to the rear top and base rails as well.

Using sash clamps, or a soft rope, pull the pillars tight to the rear top rail, and fit the pre-sprayed rear top corner

Lining up for the rear coach bolts.

Squaring up the side frames using the doors before refitting the rear pillar brackets.

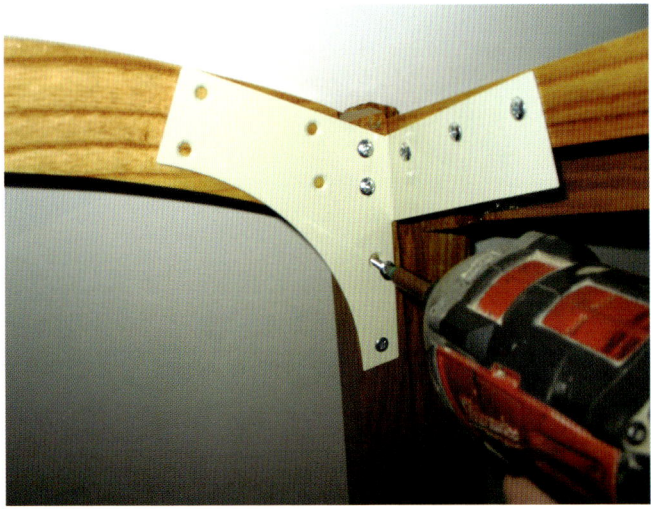

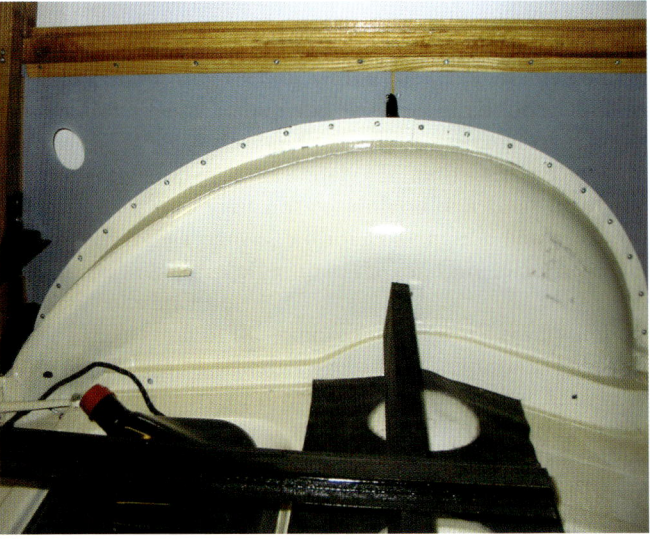

Lined up and bolted into place.

brackets. While everything is being held firmly and squarely in place, and this could easily mean with the aid of lengths of wood wedged against the garage wall, mark and drill the rear pillar for the rear door hinges. Be patient and take time over this task as it needs to be accurately done, particularly as there is little room for adjustment later. Remember to fit the ply packing pieces between the rear pillar and the metal rear corner bracket. These are important, as they allow the space for the door mechanism to fit behind the metal cross bar of the load bay floor. There is a pre-drilled hole in the top of the corner bracket for a round-headed screw. When this is fitted, it helps to hold the rear pillars in place.

With the holes carefully drilled, the hinges can now be bolted to the rear pillars. The lower bolts which pass through the securely fixed metal corner bracket help secure the pillars. The doors can be removed, leaving the hinges in place on the rear pillars.

This section of work is completed by fitting round-headed screws through the metal wheel arch flange into the wood. Normally the flange will be pre-drilled, but as each of the screws has to go through the aluminium side panel, it is advisable to drill some pilot holes. The screws should be fitted about every 100mm (4in).

Note: Don't be too alarmed about what the roof looks like when lining up the wood frame. There is an automatic tendency for the aluminium roof to twist to one side if it has been left in place while the work is being done. It is important to get the wood frame square and totally secure, before turning attention to the roof.

TACKLING THE ROOF AREA

Before attaching the roof, the headlining support beams, with headlining attached, need to be fitted into place. Whether the original headlining, or a replacement one, is being fitted, the process of fitting it to the wood roof rails is much easier if it is done off the car. The roof rails can then be screwed into position in the rebates in the cant rail. It is then best to roll up the loose headlining, cover it in plastic and tape it out of the way, ready for final fitting later. This also has the advantage of keeping it clean as other work progresses.

Lining up the roof is made easier, if the front of the roof is only loosely bolted to the front cab. This allows it to be pulled over the rear top rail and tacked into place. The front bolts will easily stretch the roof back into place, once it is fully tacked along the rear top rail. A key point here is that it is important to make sure that the roof covers most of the wood on the rear top rail. By the time the roof gutter is fitted, no wood on this rail should be visible.

When starting the process of fitting the roof, it is very likely that the roof will be twisted to one side, so it will be easier if there are two people available to help. With one person pushing to position the roof correctly, the other will be free to put a holding tack into one side about 100mm (4in) from the rear corner. It is important to only hammer the tack in far enough for it to hold the roof straight. A pair of gloves with a non-slip palm will be required for the next phase of this task. Grip the rear of the roof panel with your fingers, and using your thumbs, pull the centre over the rear top rail until the wood is almost covered. While this is being held in place, the second person should tack the roof in place. Once secure, attention can then switch to the front where a few bolts can be tightened. Sufficient space needs to be left for the fitting of the T-rubber. A couple of short off-cuts put into place will help. Now the rest of the tacks can be hammered in. The holes in the roof are countersunk about every other hole, so these can be used to hammer the tack heads in for a flush fit.

FITTING THE ROOF GUTTERING

With the roof firmly fixed, and hopefully ripple free, attention can turn to fitting the roof guttering. At first this may seem a daunting task, but it is not as difficult as one might imagine, provided a few straight-forward instructions are followed carefully. The first step is to get the drip moulding the right way up. Looking at the end cross section, it can be clearly seen that the top section has been moulded so that it can fold down easily.

Begin by holding the 7ft (213cm) length of gutter in place along the side, and mark where a cut is to be made, to allow for the T-rubber. As the T-rubber will probably not be in place at this stage, a section of the new piece which will be fitted later can be offered up.

First section of guttering tacked in place. The cut out for the T-rubber is clearly visible.

Note: Originally no sealant was put between either the roof and the gutter, or the gutter and the roof. Very occasionally this did cause problems, with water getting through the tack holes and causing rot in the cant rail. A thin bead of sealant can be placed along the roof, but care must be taken not to use a silicone based sealant. Unless extreme caution is exercised, this can get on the roof and cause an adverse reaction with the paint.

With the new section of guttering held exactly in place, and tightly butted up to the front cab, the first tack can be put in place; 20mm (about 3/4in) from the front is ideal. Using a very thin drill bit (about 2mm), drill through the gutter and roof at the same time, to a depth of about 5mm (3/16in). Start the tack, and then use a punch to take it all the way in. A second tack should be added about halfway along to help hold the guttering in place. Working from front to back, put a tack in about every 100mm (4in). On the rear corner put the last two tacks about 25mm (1in) apart.

Now for the tricky bit! Start bending the gutter around the corner to about 145 degrees. The aluminium will have started to stretch, and the lower lip will be clearly exposed. Before going any further, cut out a section of about 25-30mm (1in plus) of the bottom lip on the apex of the bend. The edges will need filing over but this can be done later.

With this cut-out completed, continue working the gutter round the corner. Bend and tack as you go round, but use a metal or wooden drift to get the gutter flat to the roof, rather than using the tacks which will tend to pull through the soft

Fitting the roof guttering.

WOODWORK – FITTING THE FRAME

alloy. Ignore the top section of the gutter at this time unless it is restricting access for the tacks. If this happens, use the drift to tap it gently upwards. Once around the corner, it is simple to follow the line of the roof and put in the rest of the tacks. Aim to get an overlap on the roof and rear top rail of about 1 or 2mm. This way a neater edge will be achieved once the rear door seal is fitted.

Join gutter at the rear in the centre.

Dressing the top section of the gutter moulding over the tack heads.

done is to patiently dress the gutter in, with small wooden or metal drifts, until it fits flat to the roof. If a perfect fit cannot be achieved using this method, a little filler will solve the problem. Finally file the sharp edges of the lower lip, cut out earlier, and using a fine emery cloth, sand and smooth. With all these tasks completed, the guttering and the roof can be prepared for etch priming and painting.

ALMOST FINISHED

With the frames securely fitted and the roof on, the Traveller body is finally back in a recognisable shape. Most of the remaining tasks are mainly to do with refitting other components. Provided time and care was taken on the preparation of the wood frames, metal panels, and the lining up of the frames, the remaining work should be straightforward.

DOORS: FINAL FITTING

The gutters are supplied slightly over-length. It is best to cut each gutter with a hacksaw or grinder at the centre of the rear of the roof. It is advisable to cut at a slight angle so that the second section will fold neatly on top. A neat join in the centre makes all the difference. Once in position, all that remains is to fold the top lip down and tidy the corners. A 150mm (6in) piece of slightly rounded wood or plastic is ideal for this. The best results are achieved by moving from front to back, gently tapping it down a little at a time. If too much force is applied all at once, it will ripple. Once the tack heads are covered, do not be tempted to give one last heavy tap with the hammer. The tack heads will show through. Instead, move the piece of wood or plastic up to the top grove in the moulding, and tap the gutter tight to the roof.

The main problem encountered will be on the corners. Care needs to be exercised here, as the aluminium will have been stretched. It will sit proud of the roof. All that can be

As the doors have already been pre-fitted, then this stage should be fairly simple. For ease of pre-fitting, the doors will have been in their bare state. If this is still the case, it is worth hanging them again, and checking that nothing has moved and that they fit perfectly squarely in the space. Any final trimming, possibly on the top corners or down the outer lip

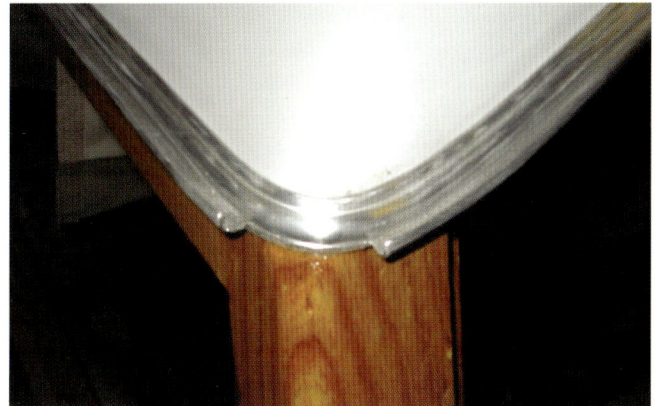

Fitting panels and glass to the rear doors.

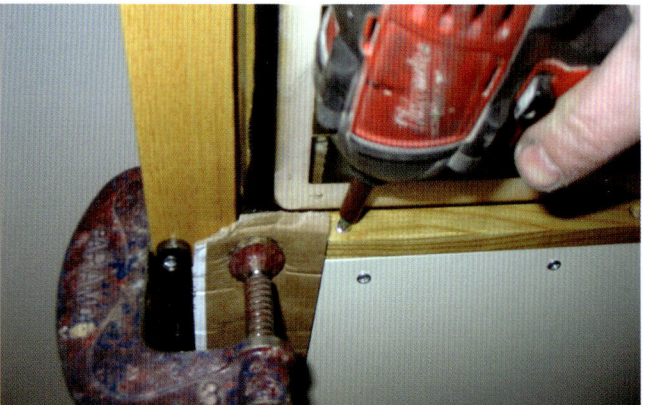

Window fillets trimmed to size and fitted to hold the glass.

of the hinge pillars, should be completed before work commences on preserving and varnishing the wood. At the same time the wood fillets which hold the glass in should be trimmed, pre-fitted, and sanded to be flush with the inside of the door.

Once the doors have been preserved and the final finish applied, thoughts can turn to fitting the aluminium panels, the windows and the door furniture. The same method used on the sides should be adopted for the fitting of the panels. Use a flat section of wood to compress caulking sealant and ensure the panel fits flat to the frame.

The glass is fitted by applying sealant round the inside of the window frame, and then slotting the glass into the top rebate. Use the pre-trimmed wood fillets and a G clamp to push the glass into place, and squeeze out any excess sealant. Once the glass and fillets are correctly located, screw them into place.

FITTING THE DOOR STAY MECHANISM

Assuming all the rods and brackets have been cleaned up, all that has to be done is fit the L-shaped brackets into place. Fit the bottom two where the pre-drilled holes are in the aluminium panel. Follow this by fitting the top one about 50mm (2in) from the top of the door. It is advisable to pre-drill for the small round-head screws, to prevent splitting the thin sections of wood. The final upper bracket has to be fitted as the mechanism is slid into place. Slide the bottom rods followed by the top rods through the holes in the brackets, making sure that the remaining top bracket has been put on the rod ready for fitting. Line up the centre of the mechanism with the holes in the panel, and then work out where the remaining bracket needs to be fitted.

Brackets for door mechanism.

WOODWORK – FITTING THE FRAME

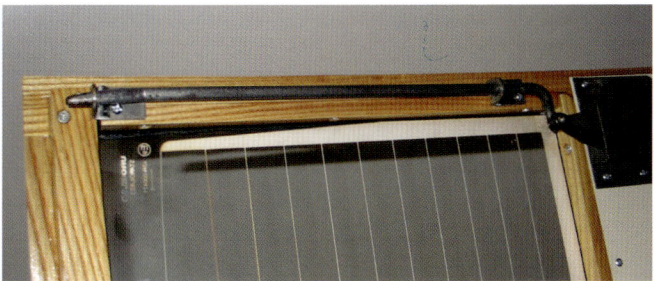

Door handle mechanism fitted.

It's a tight fit, but it is just possible to drill a pilot hole and get the screws into place before finally screwing the lock assembly into place. The door handle pushes through from the outside and is held by two screws, plus an extra screw and washer on the inside. A little drop of oil may be needed to allow the whole mechanism to work freely. The striker plate needs to be fitted to the left-hand door and the chrome badges to the right-hand door panel. At the top of the centre pillar on the left-hand door is a small L-shaped piece of metal, held in place with two very small screws. The tail of the L sits on top of the centre door seal, so it is supported when the doors are shut together. Its purpose is to make sure the centre of the doors line up at the top, and press evenly against the top rail door seal. It is better to fit both the centre door seal, a flat section of rubber about 12mm by 4mm (1/2in by 5/32in), and the metal striker once the doors are on and perfectly aligned.

With the doors fully assembled, it is time to fix them to the wood frame. Attach each of the doors to the pre-positioned hinges on the rear pillar. Loosely fit the spring washers and nuts. For ease of availability, and also due to their slightly small dimensions, plated M6 coach bolts 50mm (2in) long are preferable. With the nuts still loose, line up the doors and if necessary, wedge them into position so that there is an even gap all round, including the centre. It must be remembered that a quadrant rubber seal has to be fitted later on. It must *not* be fitted before hanging the doors.

Once the correct alignment has been achieved, with an even gap all round, tighten all the nuts on the hinges. The doors should now work freely. If the rods of the door stay mechanism do not exactly line up with the sockets in the rear top and base rails, then carefully adjust them by bending the end of the rods.

If the roof has been sprayed, the rear door seals can now be fitted. First cut the quadrant sections to length and mitre into the corners. Fit the top and bottom sections first and the sides last. Use an impact adhesive which can be brushed on, or an industrial-strength spray adhesive. Follow the instructions and allow the surfaces to dry for the recommended time before fitting. The door seals must fit exactly into place first time, as once in position they cannot be re-adjusted. Repeat the process with the flat strip in the centre door pillar and fit the metal striker plate. Finally, use a clean cloth with white spirit to remove any glue from the door seals and surrounding wood.

Finally, fit the rear door handle.

Door top striker plate fitted over the door seal.

Fitting the correct door seal and the top bracket to the left hand door. Essential to ensure leak proof doors.

Shut the doors onto the new door seals. Both doors need to be closed at the same time. They will meet about 200mm (8in) from the shut position. Gentle pressure will get them to spring shut, and the door handle can then be turned to lock them in place. With the new seals fitted the doors will be tight fit, so a knee at the bottom and a hand at the top will be required to get the door stay rods to locate properly. It is best to leave the doors in the closed position overnight to let them bed in, and for the glue on the seals to dry completely. It may take a couple of weeks for the doors to bed in properly. However, this is much better than having doors which rattle and leak just a few months down the line.

FITTING THE CAB ROOF T-RUBBER

With all spray work completed the T-rubber can be fitted. The present quality and design of these extrusions makes it a much easier job than it was a few years ago. First remove all of the bolts which go through the front top rail. Then loosen the top four front pillar bolts. By using an old chisel and a wooden wedge, it should be possible to open up the gap sufficiently to allow the new rubber to slot into place. Start at one end by cutting the T-rubber at about 45 degrees. Push down tight to the roof guttering, and start working towards the centre. Once the first half is in place, fit the first two bolts. Due to the fact that the tail of the T-rubber is longer than it needs to be, it can be gripped with a set of mole grips from the inside of the car and pulled down tight. To complete the task, the mole grips need to be used under each hole to pull the rubber into position, so that a hole can be drilled through and a bolt inserted. As this process progresses across the roof, the T-rubber will become tightly sealed to the roof. Not only is no sealant required but it is not advisable. Provided the metal surfaces are clean and flat a perfect seal will be formed. Sealant is not required. In fact it is actively discouraged.

Careful cutting to length is required in order to ensure a good fit against the guttering. Once all the bolts are in place

A correctly fitted cab roof T rubber looks and seals better.

WOODWORK – FITTING THE FRAME

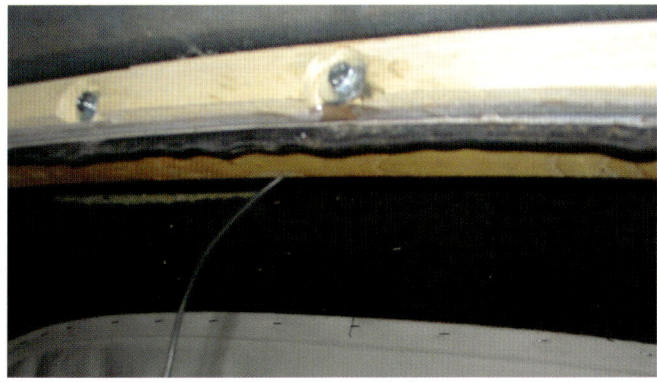

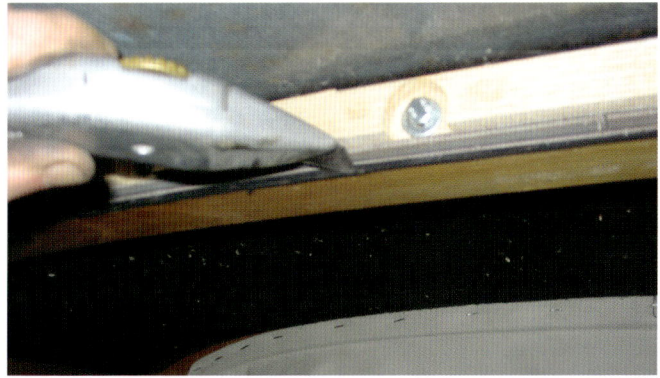

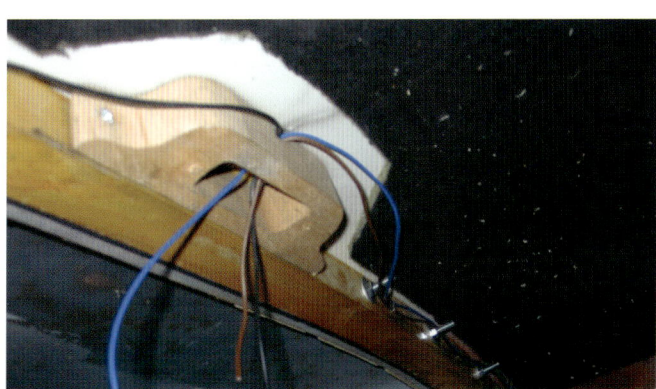

Trim the inside T rubber and refit interior light wires.

and tightened, there is still a tendency for the final 50mm (2in) of the rubber to lift. Working from inside the car, pull the end of the T-rubber tight to the roof and then, as was done in the factory, use a flat screwdriver to turn the metal lip of the cab roof to lock it into place. If the rubber is still not seated properly, a dab of black rubber adhesive may be required to give permanent seal. Remember to re-tighten all the front pillar bolts.

FITTING THE WINDOWS

Fitting the windows should be a relatively quick job, as the upper runners are already in place. Fitting the windows is the exact reverse of taking them out. The outer runner, which is easily identified by a bright stainless steel beading, should be held under the outer front window and lifted into place. Pre-cut the window runner to the correct length, and if it is not already slotted with drain holes. then drill 6mm (1/4in) holes about every 150mm (6in). Once the window and the runner are correctly positioned, a couple of screws at each end should suffice to hold the runner in place and stop it lifting at the ends.

Re-fitting the rear windows with new window runners.

> **FOREMAN'S TIP**
> Do not use any sealant but hold the runner tight to the side of the waist rail, and insert the screws at a slight angle towards the outside of the wood. This will prevent the screws from going into the rebated channel in the wood and causing future problems.

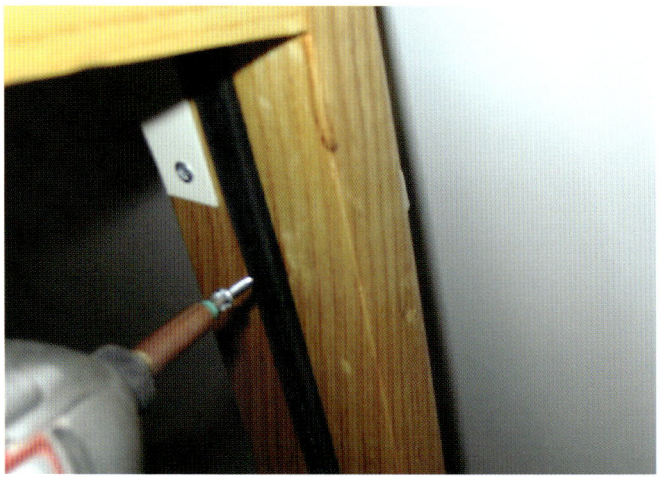

Fill the gap between the waist rail and rear pillar joint with a flexible sealant.

Lifting the windows into place and securing the runners.

The joints at the front and rear of the waist rail, where the tenons go into the front and rear pillars, allow water to get into the joints and eventually cause rot. Before putting the windows in, fill these gaps with a non-setting caulking sealant. Do not use silicone. Although it remains flexible, the seal will break down and allow water through. Previously Dum Dum was the best product for this purpose, but unfortunately it is becoming increasingly difficult to get hold of.

The inner rear window is fitted in the same method as before. Unlike the outer runner, it is a standard black runner without the stainless steel bead. Before fitting, drill drain holes if required. This runner extends the full length of the waist rail, but stops and tucks under the metal fillet which is screwed to the inside of the front of the waist rail capping. As it is held firmly at the front by this fillet, only a single screw is required at the rear. When fitting this screw, position it so that it goes into the high point of the wood between the rebated channels. The final sections of runner which need to be fitted, are the two uprights at the front and rear. Two screws in each of these should be sufficient to hold them in place.

The inner waist rail capping which helps hold the windows in place needs to be fitted. However, before doing this it is advisable to fit the vinyl side panels into place, and if new grey Hardura matting is being fitted on the load bay floor and inner wheel arches, then this too should be done beforehand.

WOODWORK – FITTING THE FRAME

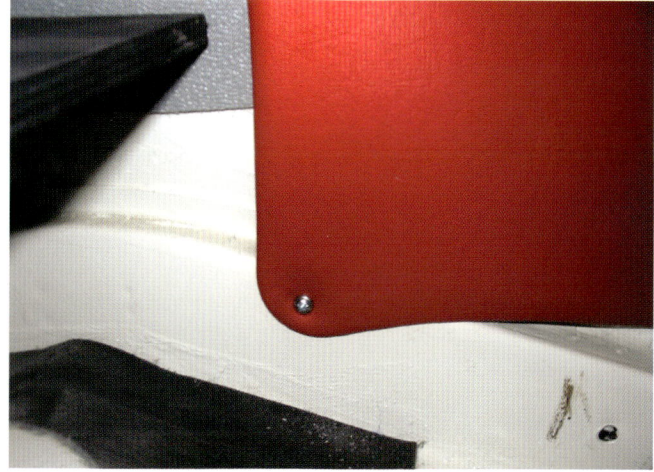

trimming is required, always cut from the front end, so that the pre-drilled holes for the door stays and seat brackets remain in the correct place. Once trimmed to the correct length, offer it up and, if a new capping is being used, mark where the cut-out for the window catch needs to be. To do this, push the rear window fully into place and then mark where the catch should slot in. Different types of catches were fitted during the Traveller's long production run. For instance, early cars have flip-over catches fitted. The same process applies regardless of the type of catch fitted.

The vinyl panels need to be fitted before the waist rail cappings.

FITTING THE WAIST CAPPING RAIL

Begin by fitting the front pillar capping into place. This will need to be taken out again to fit the headlining, but it needs to be there in order to judge the length of the capping rail. Offer the wood rail up and mark where it needs trimming. If

A small black L-shaped bracket with a slot in the top has to be fitted to the inside of the waist rail. The capping rail has to be rebated to allow for the thickness of this bracket. Mark on the inside of the capping rail where it will sit, and use a large Forstner drill bit or a router to rebate the wood, making sure that where the rebate shows at the top of the capping, it is no wider than the metal bracket. With this bracket screwed to the inside face of the waist rail, the window can now be locked, and the capping rail should sit neatly over it. Occasionally a small amount of wood may need to be removed from the top edge of the capping to allow it to sit high enough. Make sure all bare wood exposed by the rebating is varnished.

The capping is now ready to fit. If the metal fillet is not already attached, then fit it now. It needs to be fixed with four small screws, no longer than the thickness of the wood. Once fitted, run two beads of caulking sealant along the inside face of the waist rail about 35mm (1½in) apart. Having two beads of sealant helps to make sure that the capping sits flat. Screw into place with the raised countersunk screws provided. The seat bracket and rear door stay bracket can now be fitted.

Cappings fitted.

FITTING THE REAR HEADLINING

Before fitting the last of the inner capping rails, the headlining has to be fitted. If the original headlining is being refitted, this is a pretty straightforward task. As the roof rails are already in position with the headlining attached, having been fitted before the roof went on, it is just a matter of inserting five screws through the rear ply stiffener into the rear top rail and then, starting in the middle at the front, tensioning the headlining and stapling it to the ply packer held under the front top rail bolts. Before doing this, trim any excess off the new T-rubber. Check that the earth wire for the interior light has been reconnected, and that the remaining wires have been passed through the slot in the lining. Once the headlining has been evenly tensioned, from front to back, staple the sides to the cant rail. Pull the sides of the lining as low as possible before stapling. This will ensure that when the cappings are screwed into place, they will pull any remaining creases from the material. Fit the cant rail cappings level with the bottom of the window runners. In most cases the rearmost screw will need pre-drilling through the rear metal corner bracket. The final task is to attach the wires and screw the interior light into place. If a new headlining is being fitted, then it is a case of following the manufacturer's instructions.

REAR LIGHTS

Refitting the rear lights, including rear flashers if fitted, is simply a reversal of the stripping-down process. It is a good idea to use new rubber boots and bulb holders. With the wires already identified when they were removed, it should be simply a matter of inserting them into the holders, checking that the bulbs are working and then screwing the holders in place, using ¾in number 6 screws. Before fitting the lenses, the addition of a thin smear of Vaseline on the rubber boot will make fitting easier, and help to create a watertight seal. This also applies to fitting the outer chrome bezel. This can be a fiddly job. It is best done using a small blunt screwdriver. With one edge of the bezel in place, slide the screwdriver around the lip of the rubber pushing the bezel in to place. Finally fit the reflector, which should be located just above the lower hinge, or below the hinge on earlier cars without separate rear flashers.

The rear lights back in place.

WOODWORK – FITTING THE FRAME

FINISHING TOUCHES

The wood replacement is now complete apart from a few finishing touches. Final tasks include trimming off any caulking sealant which may have squeezed out, wiping down with white spirit, and applying a final top coat to the wood, after a light rub down with fine sandpaper. 320 or 400 grit is ideally suited. This final coat will cover the join between wood and sealant.

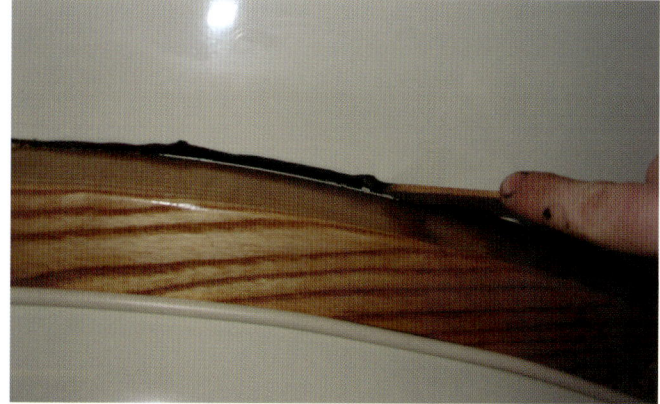

Clean off the excess sealant before adding a final protective top coat to the wood.

The original factory finish to the lower front pillar bolts was a light brown paint. With modern zinc plating, this is not necessary for protection. so this is optional. However, the final top coat should cover the edges of the washer to stop water getting into the bolt hole.

Depending on how the welding has been completed behind the B-post, it may be necessary to fit a closing panel. This is a small metal plate the length of the foot rail which butts up to the rear inner sill. It is held in place with three screws. It is basically a splash plate covering the gap between the wood of the foot rail and the boxing plate extension. It is beneficial if it wraps round the end of the foot rail, and is sealed with a seam sealer or under seal. This will prevent water thrown up by the wheels of the car from getting between the wood and the boxing plate. Although the factory-fitted closing panels were screwed into place, welding on a more substantial plate is an option. However, if this is done provision needs to be made for a drain hole to be incorporated in the panel.

That's it. Job done! Provided the maintenance tips described in the wood finishing section are followed, it should be many years before any problems arise.

Finished at last and well worth the effort.

117

CHAPTER 11
WOODWORK – RESTORATION AND PARTIAL REPLACEMENT

Assembling the Frame. The joints and fixings that cannot be seen.

Not all Travellers warrant full wood replacement. Some may require the fitting of a couple of new wood sections to provide a new lease of life. Even if the woodwork has been regularly maintained, there will come a time when more extensive restoration is required, and a complete strip back of the woodwork becomes necessary. In preparation for this process, the windows will need to be taken out and the rear doors taken off. All the rear light fittings and the lower front pillar bolts will also need to be removed. The removal of all these items has been described in chapter 8.

In most cases, the best way to remove the original finish is by using a hot air gun and a good quality scraper. A long-handled scraper with a reversible tungsten blade is preferable, and these are readily available at good hardware outlets. This type of scraper allows good leverage and control. Begin by softening the finish with the hot airgun. Keep it moving and do about 150-200mm (6-8in) at a time. The scraper will take the varnish, oil, and most other finishes off in one hit, and will leave a smooth clean finish. Follow this with a light sand-down to provide sufficient key for the new replacement finish. Areas which have become black or stained will need extra work. More scraping and more sanding will be required. Although it is possible to use a two-part bleach on the wood, this is not advisable. There are a number of reasons for this. Firstly, it is not effective because if the staining is on the surface it will scrape off, and if it is deeper, and coming from inside the wood, the bleach will only deal with the top surface. As soon as you apply a finish, the staining will come back. Secondly, the bleach will weaken the surface of the wood, and as a consequence the durability of the chosen finish will be reduced.

If the wood has previously been coated in an acrylic water-based product, then the hot airgun will not be effective. Neither will sanding. The only way to remove this type of finish is by using paint stripper. It is essential to protect all paintwork if this method is adopted. No matter which product is used, follow the instructions meticulously. Apply sparingly, and thoroughly neutralise the wood surface after scraping off the old finish.

The various types and application of the finishes available has been dealt with in the wood finishing section (chapter 9). Whatever finish is chosen, make sure the wood is thoroughly dry, and that its preparation is to the highest standard possible. The eventual standard of finish achieved will be totally dependent upon the results of the preparation which has gone before. To this end, make sure the drain holes in the middle rail are cleaned out, and if necessary re-drill them to give a clean edge. Plug the bottom of the drain holes as described earlier, and fill with preservative and basecoat. Leave overnight to soak in, topping up if necessary, before continuing with the re-finishing process.

Once the wood finishing is complete, re-fit the windows with new runners and replace the cappings, doors, and lights, as described previously (chapter 10). If the job has been done properly, then apart from regular annual maintenance, it should not be necessary to go through this process for another eight to ten years.

This whole process should take about a week, depending on the weather and what facilities are available. In Britain, it is advisable to do this work between May and August, as outside of this timeslot the risk of trapping damp in the wood increases, as does the drying time of the exterior wood finish.

REPLACEMENT OF INDIVIDUAL WOOD SECTIONS
Fitting individual replacement sections into the wood frame is within the scope of the amateur home restorer. Some sections are easier to fit than others, but provided you have access to a reasonable selection of woodworking tools and adopt a patient and methodical approach, excellent results can be achieved. It is important to realise that with the passage of time, most Travellers will have had full sets of

WOODWORK – RESTORATION AND PARTIAL REPLACEMENT

wood or individual sections replaced previously, so when new sections are purchased, it cannot be assumed that they are going to be a perfect fit. Equally important is the need to objectively appraise the condition of the sections the new piece of wood is going to be fitted to. If they are not sound, dry and rot free, it may be time to reconsider.

The two main sections which usually need replacing are the middle rail and the rear pillar. Fortunately these are also the sections which are easiest to fit. Basic instructions for fitting the individual sections, apart from the cant rail, are detailed below. Replacing cant rails is a much more involved, as it requires the guttering to be removed and the roof to be separated from the wood. As a rule of thumb, if more than three sections need replacing, and if one of them is the cant rail, then it is best to fit a complete assembled side. It will be easier, look better, and add long term value to the vehicle.

For a more in-depth look at removing windows and doors, lights and fixings, refer to the main text for wood dismantling (chapter 8).

REPLACING A WAIST RAIL

First remove all screws from the waist rail capping, including rear door stays and rear seat brackets. Prise the capping away from the waist rail. This will probably have to be done gradually, as the sealant will have hardened off over the years.

Once the capping has been removed, the windows together with the lower window runners can be lifted out, using a lever under the runners. The window catch brackets may have to be removed from the waist rail, depending on the year of the Traveller. At this stage, the front pillar capping should be removed by taking out the four securing screws and undoing the seat belt bolt, if fitted.

Lift out the trim panels below the waist rail, after first removing the two retaining screws. The first is located where the two panels join; the rear seat base covers the second. The screws holding the metal panels to the waist rail should now be visible, and should be removed together with the securing screws at each end of the waist rail – two in the rear pillar and two in the front pillar.

The waist rail can now be removed. This is more easily done, if a saw cut is made through the rail either side of the centre upright, and close to the rear and front pillars. Two large sections can now be lifted away and the remaining wood can be chiselled out carefully, thus protecting the sections not being replaced.

To fit the new waist rail, which should have first been given a suitable protective coating on the inside faces, apply glue to the joints and insert the rear end into the mortice of the rear pillar. Then pull the front end down from above and inside the car. It will be a tight fit but avoid the temptation to shorten the waist rail, except on the tenon which slots in behind the front pillar. It is helpful if this tenon is reduced by about 1/2in (13mm). It will be necessary to bend away the metal partly covering the front pillar joint. This is not a difficult task, and it can easily be bent back once the waist rail is in place.

Screws now need to be put into the joints and along the length of the rail to hold the panels in place. Sealant needs to be applied between the metal panels and the waist rail. It is important to make sure the panels fit tightly into the rebate on the waist rail. Failure to do so may make it difficult to replace the windows. If drain holes have not already been drilled in the waist rail, this should be done now. Using a 1/4in drill, five holes should be drilled in each rebate. It is also worth drilling the new lower window runner every 4in (100mm) as well. To achieve a tight joint between the waist rail and the centre upright, it may be necessary to trim the centre upright. A screw through the waist rail from above will also help.

After replacing the windows, fit the waist rail capping, having first applied a bead of sealant. A continuous, unbroken bead is required. Care needs to be taken over this, as any breaks will let water in, especially at each end of the rail. It is important that all joints are dry before fitting the waist rail, and that a quality wood preservative is applied to protect both new and old wood. Provided the job is completed with care and patience, the new wood section should remain problem free for many years.

REPLACING A REAR PILLAR

First remove the rear door, which is attached by four bolts through the rear hinges. The nuts should come undone, but if they are rusted on, then use a grinder to cut through the bolts. The door stay will also have to be removed before the door can be lifted off. The rear lights and reflector must now be removed, taking note and marking which wire does what. It is sensible to replace any rusted light holders and perished rubber light bodies as necessary.

Although it is not totally necessary, it makes the job easier if the rear side window is out. To do this, follow the instructions as shown in the main wood dismantling text (chapter 8). The rear part of the headlining needs to be removed to give access to the rear corner brackets. This is easily done by removing the screws from the rear and side top cappings, and removing as many staples from the headlining as required. The screws in the rear corner bracket will now be visible and can be taken out.

At the base of the pillar there is a large coach bolt that will be difficult, if not impossible, to remove. The wood around it will need to be chiselled away. The bolt can be cut off after the pillar has been removed. On the inner face of the pillar, in the region of the rear lights, there are two screws through a metal bracket and a ply packing piece. The upper one is easily removed, but the lower one may have to be removed using a hammer and chisel.

The only remaining screws are at the top of the rear pillar. Unfortunately, these are not accessible without removing the

The joints and screws that you can't see when the wood is on the car

FOREMAN'S TIP

Make sure the required distance of 14⅜in (365mm) is left between the faces of the cant and waist rail to which the window runners are attached, so as to allow room for the glass. Remember to apply sealant to the rear quarter panel, before tapping the rear pillar fillet into place. Use a portable power screwdriver if possible. This makes the job much easier. Always use 'pozi' zinc plated screws where possible.

guttering and roof. To avoid doing this, cut the pillar just below the roof and above the waist rail, and lift this section away. What remains can carefully be chiselled out of the roof area. Care needs to be taken not to damage the rear top rail and the cant rail. The lower section of the pillar needs to be carefully broken away from the middle rail and rear wheel arch. Greater success can be achieved, if the area closest to the joint is chiselled away first. The remaining wood can be removed with a hard tap, using a mallet.

After removing the pillar, clean up and treat the wood around the sections remaining on the car with Cuprinol Complete Wood Treatment or an equivalent product. Make sure these areas are thoroughly dry before fitting the new section. If time is a problem, a hot air gun or hair dryer can be used to speed things up. The new pillar should also be treated and finished, particularly in the areas that will be covered when fitted.

To fit the new rear pillar, first make sure the top is chamfered sufficiently to slot neatly into the roof between the cant and rear top rail joints. Repeated trial fits and trimming will be required before a snug fit is achieved. Check that the waist rail tenon fits into the rear pillar. Do not be too concerned about the angle of the joint at this stage. This will automatically become correct when the top and bottom joints are pulled into place.

Apply glue to the joints. Modern PU (polyurethane) glue is best, as it expands into the joint and is waterproof and flexible. It also works even when the wood is damp. With the pillar in place, use G clamps to hold both the bottom of the pillar tight to the rear wheel arch joint, and the top of the pillar to the cant rail. The easiest way of clamping the top is to first clamp a small block of wood to the outside of the cant rail. This leaves room to get to the inside of the cant rail and fit a screw through into the rear pillar.

At the base of the pillar the coach bolt can now be fitted, and screws can be put through into the rear wing and rear wheel arch into the pillar. The three screws at the waist rail and rear pillar joint can be inserted in the same places as they were removed. Leave overnight to allow the glue to dry. Then remove any excess glue, trim the joints, and apply the chosen finish. To hang the rear door, hold it in place and mark through the hinges. Allow clearance for the rear door seal. Drill through the rear pillar making sure the top holes locate in the inner rebate.

This next step may not be necessary if a tight fit has already been achieved. However, if a tighter fit is required to hold the roof closer to the rear pillar, drill three small holes through the guttering and countersink. Insert three screws and cover the heads with body filler. This can then be sanded and be touched in with paint to match. If new guttering is being fitted, tack the roof flat before fitting the new guttering strip as described earlier. Finally, fit all the trim parts that were removed.

REPLACING A B-POST (FRONT PILLAR)

Preparatory work for replacing the front pillar involves removing the inner front pillar and cant rail cappings (chapter 8). The front pillar is usually only replaced, if the foot rail is being fitted at the same time. As this section comes fully machined, drilled for the bolt holes and ready to fit, it is pretty straightforward. Remove the old section by chiselling the area around the waist rail, cant rail, and foot rail joints. With the five bolts removed, the old section will lift away. For problems removing these bolts, see main wood dismantling text (chapter 8). The remainder of the foot rail will also have to be removed, by chiselling away the area around the front joint of the wheel arch.

Before fitting the front pillar and foot rail, preserve and seal all the inside faces. Apply a caulking sealant to the front lip of the metal B-post and the front edge of the aluminium panel. Fit the new section into place. Use PU glue where it meets the cant rail, and put a screw in through the rear of the cant rail tenon and the waist rail tenon. Fit the bolts through the pre-drilled holes, preferably after applying a liberal smear of grease first. Some trimming will probably be needed at the top of the front pillar to get it to fit, and a small cut-out will be required to get it to sit under the front lip of the roof. Before fitting, make sure the new foot rail is trimmed ready to fit the bottom joint of the pillar.

The aluminium panel can now be screwed into the back of the front pillar. Make sure the screws are not over-tightened, as this may cause the aluminium panel to ripple. Refer to the section below for assistance on how to secure the panel where the screw heads cannot be accessed.

REPLACING A FOOT RAIL

Regardless of whether the front pillar or the front wheel arch sections have been replaced, the fitting of the foot rail remains the same. Having chiselled away the old section, cleaned up and prepared the metal of the boxing plate extension, and trimmed the joints to fit, the inner face and underside of the foot rail and the fillet need to be sealed and preserved. The wood section then lifts into place and is glued and then screwed from underneath. Two 3in number 10 screws are all that are needed. These should be angled slightly to make sure they go into the thickest part of the bottom of the front pillar and front wheel arch.

As the aluminium panel cannot be accessed from behind, the bottom edge of the panel needs to be secured as the foot rail is fitted. Screw the wood fillet provided into the top rebate of the foot rail, leaving enough of a gap for the lower lip of the panel to slot into. Fill this gap with black caulking sealant. As the foot rail is lifted into place, the panel will be firmly held, giving a tight fit to both the bottom of the front pillar and the wheel arch. Allow the glue time to dry. Then clean and trim the joints and sand the new wood. Preserve and add an exterior finish to match the existing wood.

WOODWORK – RESTORATION AND PARTIAL REPLACEMENT

FITTING A WHEEL ARCH REAR SECTION

This is the one wheel arch section which can be fitted relatively simply on its own. The wing does not need to be removed, and the aluminium panel needs to stay in place. However a few more woodworking tools will be required. If a rear pillar is being fitted at the same time, this needs to be installed before fitting the wheel arch section is attempted.

Remove the inner vinyl panel and remove the round-head screws, now visible, from the upright of the wheel arch flange. Chisel away the old wheel arch, making sure the sections being left in place are not damaged. The flange of the rear wing will be exposed, together with the wing piping. Leave these items undisturbed if possible, and remove only the remnants of the fixings which secured the wing to the wood. Clean all the original sealant from the aluminium panels and the inner wing flange.

Offer up the new section. It will be longer and thicker than required and work will be needed to ensure a good fit. First trim the rear face to the correct angle so that it sits flat to the rear pillar. Mark where the joint needs to be cut at the front end. This will assist in creating the tongue of the lap joint. Do not worry at this stage about the thickness of the wood. The joint may have to be trimmed several times until a perfect fit is achieved.

Once tight joints have been made at both ends of the wheel arch, remove any excess wood, so the new section is flush with the centre wheel arch and outer face of the rear pillar. Preserve and seal the inside faces, apply black caulking sealant to the aluminium panel, add glue to the joints and fit into place. The rear of the wheel arch can be clamped to the rear pillar with a G clamp, and screwed through the wing with 2½in number 10 screws and washers.

Drill a pilot hole through the flange of the wing and the wheel arch, making sure the wing piping is in the correct place. By doing this, as the screws tighten the wing piping will be trapped against the edge of the wood.

To secure the front joint, drill two pilot holes from inside the car which will come through the tongue of the centre wheel arch. This is best done before finally fitting the new section. Use 1¾in screws to pull the lap joint tight. If you are using PU type glue, then leave to dry before trimming the excess glue off and giving a final sand down.

Remove any caulking sealant that has squeezed out, before preserving and finishing the wood to match. Finally screw the wing to the wheel arch with a few 1in number 10 screws and washers, taking care to make sure the wing piping is correctly aligned.

FITTING A WHEEL ARCH FRONT SECTION

This is best done at the same time as the foot rail; otherwise part of the joint at the bottom of the wheel arch will have to be cut away. The process for fitting this section is exactly the same as for the rear section.

FITTING A WHEEL ARCH CENTRE SECTION

Due to the fact that the tongues of the lap joints of this section sit behind both the front and rear wheel arch sections, it cannot be fitted without both of them being removed. For this reason it is recommended that if this section needs replacing, then a complete wheel arch should be fitted.

FITTING A COMPLETE WHEEL ARCH

The wheel arches are available as complete glued units and, apart from applying a finish, they are ready to fit. As with fitting individual sections, remove the internal vinyl trim panels and all the screws through the upright lip of the flange panel. Any screws which will not come undone may have to be chiselled off, or have the heads removed with a grinder. The rear wing must be removed. The wing may have been fitted by using bolts or screws. In most cases they will be difficult to remove, so once again it is a case of grinding the heads off, or splitting the wood away from the car and removing the wing and wood together. Clean up all the metal work before offering up the new section. Adjust the front and rear joints as necessary, and make sure the rear face will fit flat to the aluminium panels. To achieve this, a small housing joint will need to be cut in the rear face of the wheel arch to accommodate the tongue of the centre upright which joins the waist rail and the wheel arch. If the centre upright needs replacing, now is the time to do it, as it is a simple matter of chiselling the old one away from the car and re-fitting a new one with a little sealant and a couple of screws from inside the car.

It sometimes helps to chamfer the lower inside face of the wheel arch to get it to sit flat. Once this is done, preserve and seal the inside faces, apply black caulking sealant to the aluminium panels and fit. Glue and screw the joints as previously described and use 1in number 10 round-head screws through the flange from the inside. These should be fitted about every 3in (75mm). A pilot hole will need to be drilled through the metal flange. Once the glue has dried and the wood has been cleaned and finally sanded, then add the finish to match the rest of the side. All that remains is to fit the wing piping and wing. This is covered in the main woodwork replacement text (chapter 10).

A FINAL WORD FROM STEVE

With another 20,000 words and countless more photographs and diagrams, it would have been possible to give a foolproof guide to replacing and restoring the wood on a Traveller. I hope though, that enough information has been given to point you in the right direction. Most Morris Minor owners are inherently practical, and do not need their hands held through every process. I have seen some wonderful work done by amateurs, from individual sections to full wood replacements. Time and patience are the key factors. If you are seriously worried about whether you can take on the task, then call a man who can.

> **FOREMAN'S TIP**
>
> Do not fully preserve and finish the wood before fitting, as the glue will not take to the joints. Just complete the areas which are not accessible once fitted.

MORRIS MINOR TRAVELLER – THE COMPLETE COMPANION

CHAPTER 12
TRAVELLER VARIATIONS

TRAVELLER VARIATIONS

The basic design of the Morris Minor Traveller remained virtually unchanged throughout its eighteen-year production run. Of course there were upgrades in terms of mechanical specification, interior fittings, and external styling retouches. However, the instantly recognisable, timber-framed body stayed the same on all production models. Undoubtedly there were questions asked about the potential for change or further development, particularly with regard to the ease of access to the rear seat through the front doors.

As early as 1952, the possibility of a four door Traveller was being mooted in the pages of *The Motor*, following the announcement of the Morris Oxford Series MO Traveller. A few years later, probably co-incidental with the development of the Oxford Series IV all-steel four-door Traveller in 1956, the Experimental Department at Cowley made scale models of an all-steel Traveller, based on the Minor four-door saloon. One proposal retained the rounded shape of the side window in the rear door, with the third side window and the rear end following a similar line. An alternative suggestion was to give the rear side door window a more upright line, again with a corresponding angle to the rear end.

Questions were also asked why the Traveller body had not been mounted on a separate chassis in the way that the Morris Minor light commercial vans and pick-ups had. Given the nature of these queries, it is perhaps not surprising that some enterprising individuals chose to produce some interesting variants of the Morris Minor Traveller.

One of the earliest was the Berkshire Countryman Traveller of 1956. Designed and marketed by Geoffrey Crossley Industries, based at Wallingford, near Oxford, this Traveller had a coachbuilt body on a Morris Minor light commercial vehicle (LCV) chassis. The first of the vehicles produced was based on an early Series II chassis cab which from its Berkshire registration mark dated to mid-1954. The rear body, constructed of a substantial ash frame with veneered panels, differed from the standard factory produced models in several respects. A weatherproofed and soundproofed under tray with a separate spare wheel compartment was incorporated in the body design, as was a fabric sunroof and one-piece fixed windows in the rear side panels. Rearward visibility was improved by the use of larger windows in the rear doors, and the number plate was recessed in a substantial rear ash frame, so substantial that normal bumpers were dispensed with.

Interior fittings differed too. The rear floor in the load area was covered with a rubberised cork material, toned to match the upholstery, and fitted with protecting rubbing strips to help with the loading of luggage or goods, and to avoid

This unique conversion dating from 1956 has been replicated and improved as a result of an extensive restoration. There is no other Traveller like it, with the extra door on the nearside.

The Crossley Berkshireman Traveller was built using a LCV chassis cab. A 'Countryman' version which similar in style, was produced for use as a van.

damage to the floor. The vinyl-covered seats, which were offered in a number of colours to complement the exterior colour of the vehicle, were of a different design. Both the front seats and the rear bench seat had chrome rails at the top. The front seats folded and tipped forward, to allow for access to the rear seat. This would have been a necessity in the design of this particular vehicle, given that the front doors were shorter than those fitted to the factory produced Travellers, since the Berkshire Countryman retained the shorter doors fitted to the LCV models and four-door saloons.

Given the craftsmanship and skill involved in creating this unique Traveller version, it is perhaps not surprising that it sold at a higher price than standard production Travellers. Taking account of the niche market it was aimed at, the price of £766 15s6d, which was about £60 more expensive than a De Luxe Morris Minor Traveller of the same vintage, may not have seemed that unreasonable.

The company also offered a van version of the same model. Using the Minor chassis cab, a wood-panelled rear load compartment was mounted on the standard chassis. The vehicle was supplied with a driver's seat as standard. In keeping with the custom and practice of light commercial vehicles in the 1950s, a passenger seat could be specified as an extra. The price of the Berkshire Countryman van was £586 12s3d and was not subject to Purchase Tax.

INDIVIDUAL ENTERPRISES

The suggestion that a four-door Traveller would be even more versatile and allow for easier access to the rear seat, never found favour with the designers in the Experimental Department of the British Motor Corporation, despite the 1956 model mentioned above. However, at least one enter-

A number of private individuals experimented with producing variations on the Traveller design – including this attempt at creating a four door Traveller.

THREE-DOOR TRAVELLER

Without doubt, one of the most striking and cleverly engineered alternative Travellers which still exists today, is the three-door Minor 1000 Traveller belonging to Marcus and Sparky Ward. What is even more remarkable is that this vehicle has recently undergone a total restoration during which many of features of the original design, conceived in 1957, have been improved. In addition, many non-standard upgrades have been incorporated to enhance performance, driveability, comfort levels, and safety. RMJ 920 is certainly a head turner, fully equipped to deal with the rigours of twenty-first century motoring.

While it dates from 1957, the vehicle did not come to prominence until it was offered for sale thirty years later. By then it was showing signs of wear and tear and, although interesting and available for the very modest price of £500, potential buyers, including the author, were reluctant to take on the challenge of embarking on a substantial refurbishment.

The origins of the vehicle have caused a great deal of speculation over the years, and in spite of extensive enquiries and detailed research, some elements remain a mystery. What is known is that the vehicle left the factory in 1956 as a Morris 1000 van. Within a short period of time, the van back was removed, and a purpose-built body was constructed on the LCV chassis, using official BMC drawings as a starting point. All the evidence points to this being a one-off project, undertaken by a skilled engineer with the objective of creating a traditional 'Shooting Brake' model based on the Minor Traveller concept. Key components of this individually designed vehicle were an extended chassis, the addition of a nearside rear door (much like a modern Mini Clubman!), a redesigned tailgate arrangement, and the inclusion of a metal-framed sunroof. Inside the seating arrangements were modified to include a folding split rear seat, a lowered rear floor, and individually appointed interior trim. Additional features included specially constructed storage compartments on the underside of the vehicle, and Hillman Minx rear light units.

The result was an extremely versatile vehicle some 18in (457mm) longer than the production Minor Traveller. However, due to the increased weight of the vehicle and the decision to stick to the 948cc engine and standard drive train, overall performance was compromised. It is believed that the inspiration for creating such a vehicle was its potential for use on country estates for transporting members of shooting parties, their equipment, and gundogs to and from the shooting grounds. The guns could easily enter the rear seat by means of the third door and with the sunroof open, could stand to shoot at the game. The easily accessible rear load area allowed for the storage of equipment, and for dogs to be accommodated en route to the shoot. For safety, shotguns were stored while in transit in the compartment under the vehicle. When first commissioned back in 1957, the vehicle

prising individual did modify his 1967 Morris 1000 Traveller in the late 1980s. His efforts show at least one interpretation of what could have been done to produce a four-door Traveller. It may have been practical to use, but in terms of setting a trend, it did not fire the imagination sufficiently for others to replicate the process.

In principle, the conversion involved replacing the existing Traveller front doors with all four doors from a four-door saloon. In order to achieve this, the B-posts on either side of the vehicle needed to be replaced by those from a four-door saloon, located further forward. Just how far forward, is evident by the distance from the rear edge of the front door to the joining strip between the cab and the rear roof panel!

Further structural work was needed in order to position the rear pillars or C-posts with the closing panels for the rear side doors. This necessitated removing part of the curved wheel arch ash section, prior to welding in the combined metal wheel arch and door closing panel. As the doors themselves were not changed, additional panels needed to be fabricated, in order to fill the gaps between the rounded rear quarter lights and a relocated wood upright. The back doors were retained in their original location, and the interior seating remained unchanged. A few minor adjustments to the interior trim were required to provide the finishing touches. The four-door Traveller not only provided sound dependable transport for the owner and his family for a number of years, but caused much discussion amongst fellow enthusiasts who invariably greeted the vehicle with quizzical looks.

TRAVELLER VARIATIONS

was used extensively in the county of Bedfordshire.

Now resplendent in Damask Red and fully restored, this shooting brake is a stunning example of an individually designed Traveller that has stood the test of time, and has emerged as a substantially better vehicle capable of many more years of use. However, the transition from virtual wreck, banished to a barn for eighteen years, to one of the most admired Travellers on the classic car scene has come at a cost, quite literally. It is something owner Marcus Ward chooses not to dwell on, as his passion to restore his pride and joy to its former glory which started in 2006 and was largely completed by 2008, is still ongoing. His investment has been repaid many times over with admiring glances and favourable comments, though his bank balance is considerably lower.

Undertaking such a unique restoration required the services of a knowledgeable and capable project manager. Steve Foreman of the Woodies Company, and co-author of this book, was approached. Acknowledged as the Traveller wood

The shooting brake from the offside – look no rear door! – displaying its extra length.

The car as purchased in 1998, with horizontally split tailgate.

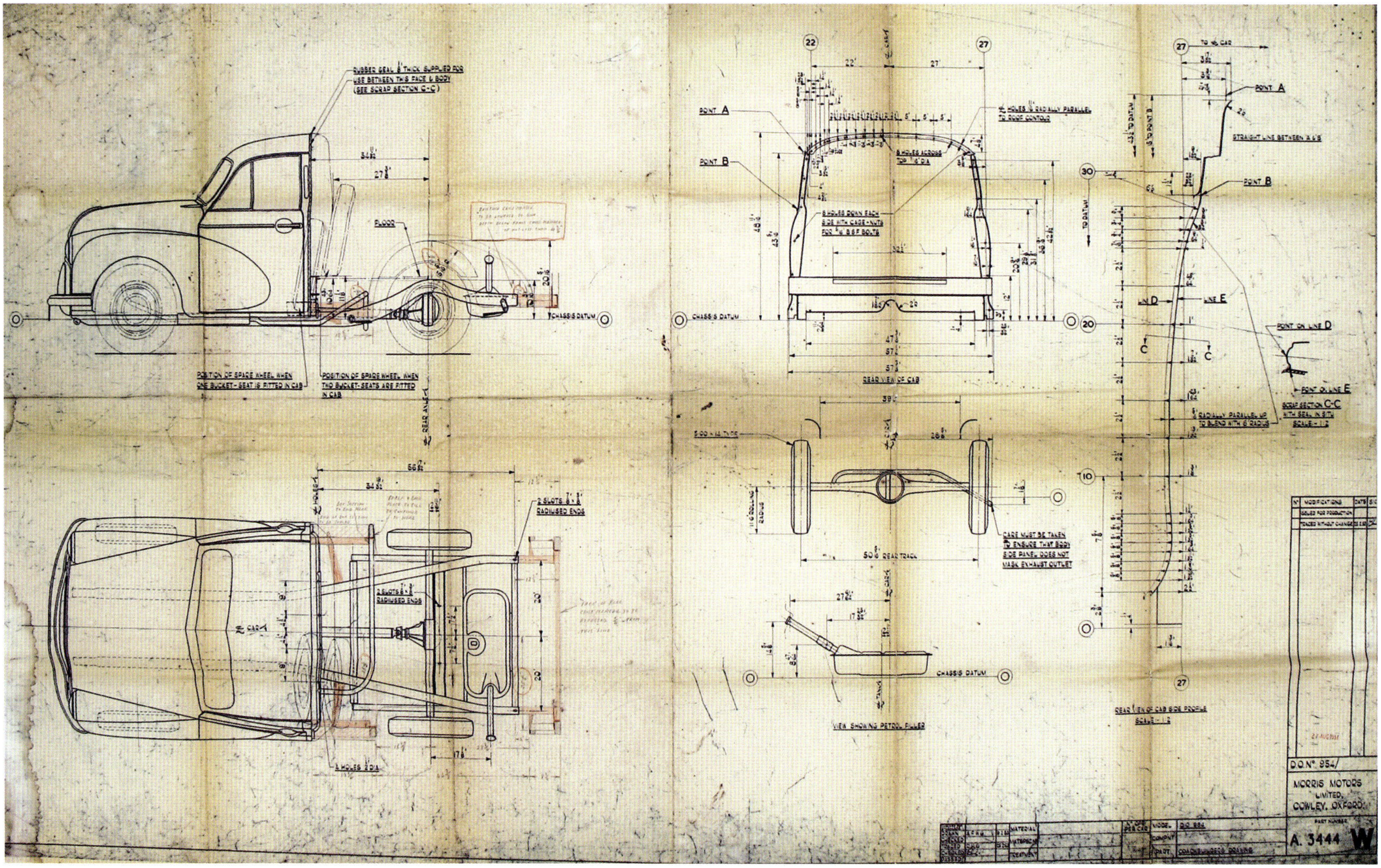

Sample of the drawings for the original design from the drawing office at Morris Motors Ltd.

guru, Steve was a natural choice to tackle the challenges associated with such a one-off restoration. Fortunately he agreed and although the project took longer than anticipated, the results speak for themselves.

As is often the case with restoration projects, there is a lot more to this than first meets the eye. The restoration of RMJ 920 was quite literally a ground-up project. Eighteen years of inactivity had taken its toll on almost every component.

The full extent of the restoration required revealed.

TRAVELLER VARIATIONS

The chassis frame was in such a poor condition that it was necessary to fabricate an all-new chassis from scratch: no mean task, even with the drawings that were available.

Recreating the wood frame was relatively straightforward, once the original had been carefully dismantled, and as many of the original pieces as possible preserved as templates for replacement parts. Recreating the framework for the third door was particularly challenging, as was the installation of a replacement sunroof which replicated the original. From the outset, the plan had been to complete the restoration to the highest professional standards, and to improve on the orig-

A new framework for the sun roof was specially commissioned.

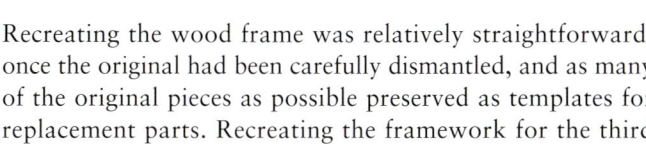

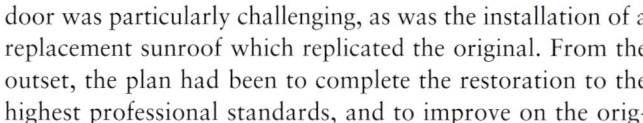

MORRIS MINOR TRAVELLER – THE COMPLETE COMPANION

Fully restored extended chassis with some additional strengthening added.

Some panels including this offside door were sourced from other vehicles. The car has the shorter front doors of the four-door saloon.

inal design where possible, while maintaining the essential character of the vehicle.

This proved to be a tall order, as the legacy of the light commercial origins of the vehicle complicated matters on several occasions. The structural rigidity of the vehicle had, over time, been weakened by the rapid deterioration of the chassis frame. In fact a new chassis had to be built and the old one dispensed with. Here the original BMC plans came into their own, and proved invaluable in clarifying the exact dimensions of the specially extended chassis as originally fabricated. The fragility of the original under-floor storage areas which originally were constructed from aluminium soon became obvious, and new stronger steel replacements were installed. Extensive repairs were carried out in the cab area, with particular emphasis on the area round the B-posts, particularly on the near side where the B-post from a four door saloon had originally been installed to accommodate the fitting of the third door.

Replicating the uniquely designed third door, and the rear tailgate with its opening window, proved to be the most challenging parts of the restoration. While remaining true to the original design, subtle, but immensely time-consuming improvements proved necessary to ensure smooth operation, as well as waterproof and rattle-free fitting. Another improvement was to ensure that the new timber frame included contoured sections which followed more closely the lines of the bodywork in the areas adjacent to the B-posts.

Other significant changes were incorporated in the rejuvenated Traveller. In deference to the increased gross weight of the vehicle, a larger 1098cc A-series engine and matching gearbox were fitted, in the hope that the improved performance over the original 948cc unit would make it easier to

TRAVELLER VARIATIONS

Purpose-made replica wooden ash frame in position.

The third door tested the skills of the professionals in order to achieve a perfect fit and smooth operation.

The original 948cc engine 'as found'. It was replaced with a larger unit.

drive and improve handling. Standard drum brakes were retained at the rear but in the interests of safety, front disc brakes were fitted. JHL Ford Sierra racing discs were chosen, and have proved to be highly efficient, improving the braking ability. Though completely refurbished with new parts, the suspension remained standard throughout with the exception of a front anti-roll bar and adjustable spax shock absorbers.

Concessions to comfort and personal preferences resulted in further amendments to the interior trim. New front seats were installed on specially modified frames suited to the LCV chassis cab. Fully adjustable tilt and slide seats complete with headrests were upholstered by Newton Commercial in grey leather. On-going improvements have resulted in the original Hillman Minx split rear seat being recovered in vinyl to match, along with the door and side panels. The fitting of a bespoke headlining, specially adapted to fit around the sliding steel sunroof, added the finishing touch to a stunning modern interior. Other refinements have included an enclosed covered rear load area courtesy of a sliding wood panel, and a high gloss finish to the inner wood panels on the opening tailgate.

Further upgrades, funds permitting, may include improvements to strengthen the rear suspension, with the installation of more robust telescopic shock absorbers. Longer term, the fitting of a more powerful engine, possibly a 1275cc A-series engine mated to a five-speed gearbox may be an option, given that the vehicle weighs 5cwt (250kg) more than a standard Morris Minor 1000 Traveller.

Whatever future modifications may be added, RMJ 920 still retains the essential characteristics of a 1956 Morris 1000 specially adapted to be a Shooting Brake. It will remain a one-off and a reminder of a bygone age when such vehicles were *de rigueur* for the country set.

Almost all the original design features of what is known to have been a 'Shooting Brake', were replicated. Some were improved. The result is a stunning, modern classic car with a real traditional feel about it.

Mechanical upgrades improved driveability and performance. A 1098cc A-series engine and Ford Sierra disc brakes were added! Note the anti roll bar fitted to the front of the car.

TRAVELLER VARIATIONS

The sun roof, originally added so that members of 'Shooting Parties' had an ideal vantage point, has been fully restored.

Though faithful to the original concept the standard of finish on the rear tailgate was markedly improved. The one piece rear window and the drop-down tail gate were innovative features in 1956 and they don't look out of place now.

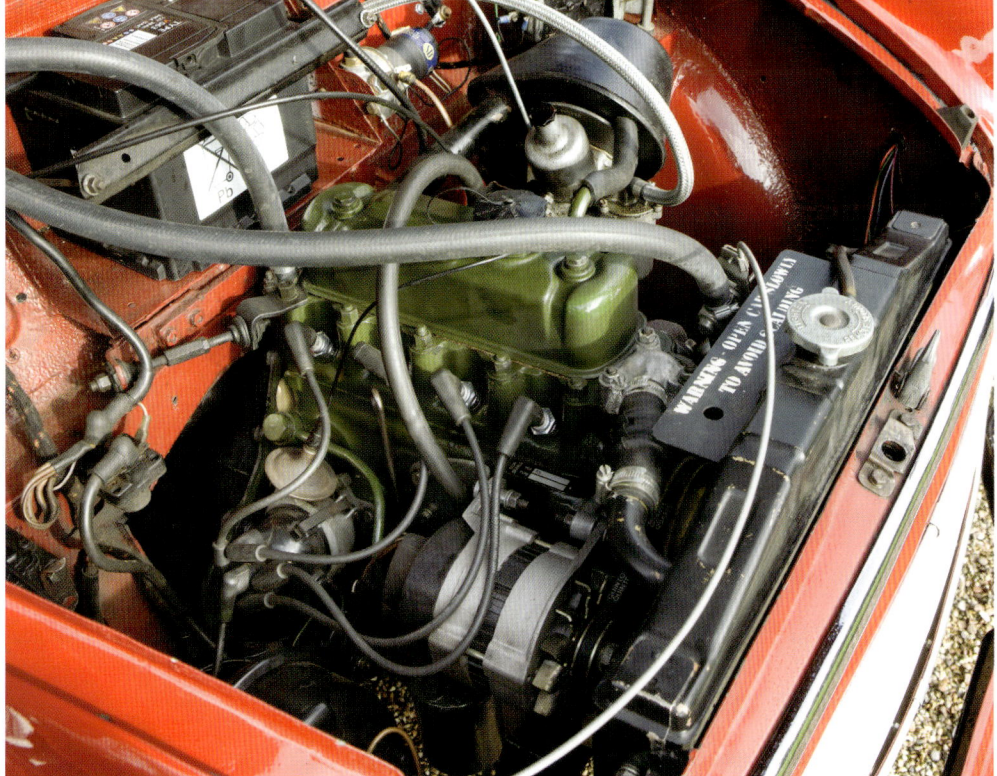

A discreet colour-coded solid blind adds an element of security to the rear storage area.

These hinges are used for the bottom half of the split tailgate.

MORRIS MINOR TRAVELLER – THE COMPLETE COMPANION

Fully adjustable front seats trimmed in leather are complemented by vinyl covered rear seats, door cards and side panels.

The dash panel retains the instrumentation added in 1956.

TRAVELLER VARIATIONS

A view through the 'Third Door'. The impressive interior trim remains true to the original trim colours and style adopted in 1956.

RMJ 920 is substantially heavier than a standard Morris Minor Traveller and is 18 inches longer!

MORRIS MINOR TRAVELLER – THE COMPLETE COMPANION

This recently restored Traveller has been adapted for use as a hearse. It entered service in 2012.

Every centimetre of the space available has been used! Features include a half rear seat, reserved for a 'bearer'.

TRAVELLER CAMPERS – AND A HEARSE...

Can you lie down in a Minor? Martin Walter of Kent tried to convince us that one could, as they showed a Dormobile conversion, based on a Minor quarter-ton van, at the Commercial Motor Show in 1954. Equipped with front and rear seats which folded flat for a makeshift double bed, it also had rear side windows and was priced at £610 5s10d including Purchase Tax, when a De Luxe Traveller cost £622 6s8d. It is not known whether they ever made a Traveller-based Dormobile, but it would have been possible.

Reg Job, a member of the original design team for the Morris Minor, along with Jack Daniels and Alec Issigonis, had the same idea. He acquired a Limeflower-coloured Minor 1098cc Traveller when he retired from British Leyland in 1971. Never one to be idle, Reg set about examining if the internal arrangements could be modified to accommodate an average-sized person wishing to sleep comfortably in the vehicle. He even went so far as to publish his drawings of the modifications necessary, for the benefit of members of the Morris Minor Owners Club.

Quite what Reg would have made of the project recently undertaken by Andrew Bywater, to prepare a Morris Minor 1000 Traveller for use as a hearse, is open to question. However, it would be safe to assume that in terms of the engineering involved, Reg would have been up for the challenge.

In what must rank as the most unusual Traveller variation of recent times, the completed hearse, which is now in service, demonstrates the versatility of the Minor Traveller.

TRAVELLER VARIATIONS

And Now For Something Completely Different!

Many unusual variations have been produced over the years such as these two American Travellers.

Randolf William's 'Real American Woodie' shows some truly amazing workmanship.

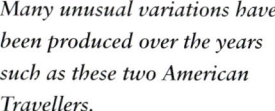

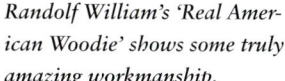

...and this is probably the shortest Traveller conversion ever!

The vehicle which has been the subject of a ground-up restoration, including a new ash frame, has been specially adapted in order to accommodate the loading deck, and seating for a bearer behind the driver. The loading deck was rescued from a Mercedes hearse which was being used as a banger racer. It was carefully cut to size to fit the Traveller, and installed along with a substantial support structure underneath. The rear seat, which has been retained in order to provide continuity of design with the front seats, had to be cut in half and be carefully modified in order to retain the original seat covering. Additional hand-made, colour co-ordinated fittings were added to provide a sense of decorum, given the intended purpose for which the vehicle was being prepared.

Needless to say, the vehicle attracts considerable interest whenever it is displayed, though most observers have no wish to ride in it just yet! – but is this 'the last word' when it comes to Minor Travellers?

CHAPTER 13
COMMERCIAL TRAVELLER CONVERSIONS

From the outset the Traveller was promoted as a dual-purpose vehicle serving the needs of the private owner and the businessman. Here a local butcher, offering a home delivery service, prepares for his round.

As we have seen, preserving the wood on the Morris Traveller requires regular attention and careful maintenance. Sadly, all too often the wood is allowed to deteriorate to the point where the vehicle fails its MOT Test, and the decision has to be made whether to replace the wood or scrap the vehicle. Back in the 1990s when Travellers were more common, this was a dilemma faced by many owners. Recognising this fact, one enterprising UK-based company came up with an alternative solution. In order to preserve the vehicle, they proposed replacing the wood with a glass fibre back, and converting the original vehicle into a Traveller-based van.

The Lincolnshire-based Custom Fibreglass Company promoted a conversion technique which would allow owners to change their ageing and deteriorating Traveller into a 'sturdy and stylish light commercial'. While stressing the need for any necessary structural repairs to be carried out to a high standard before embarking on the conversion, the plan was to provide a custom-built conversion for the owner which would create an eye-catching working vehicle, with all the characteristics expected of a van.

In effect, the aim was to provide the prospective owner with a one-piece, ribbed GRP body with an integral laminated floor which would be mounted to the rear of the Traveller cab. This specially-designed assembly was attached to the original floor, via a subframe which would be supplied as part of the package. It was assumed that any restoration of the original floor pan or chassis rails would be undertaken before fitting, and that all the timber and all aluminium panels including the roof, side panels, and rear

COMMERCIAL TRAVELLER CONVERSIONS

The Custom Fibreglass Company offered a service to convert The Traveller into a sturdy and stylish Light Commercial and produced a demonstration vehicle to promote it

door panels, would be disposed of, along with the glass in the side windows and rear doors. The preparation work even extended to removing the original wheel arches and replacing them with glass fibre ones as part of the new van back.

When the advertising literature was first released in 1998, the basic cost of converting the Traveller was £1200. The only extras required, the literature claimed, were a new set of rear light units and a different number plate light. The price included the new GRP van back along with a subframe, a one-piece rear door with hinges, and the provision of all fasteners and sealants. Also included was a fitting service which included the mounting of the petrol tank, with a new filler cap, as well as mounting the whole unit to the Traveller floor.

At extra cost, the vehicle could be primed in a two-pack finish, alternative rear light units could be fitted, and external side panels could be supplied, sign-written and fitted if required. For those wishing to dispense with metal panels on the front cab, front wings and a bonnet could also be provided in GRP. In fact any specific customer requirements could be met, and commissions could be undertaken to deal with any modifications to the GRP panel work in order to cater for any special applications.

THE TRAVAN PROTOTYPE

To promote the product, a prototype mock-up vehicle was produced and sign-written. With two different side panel designs incorporated in the same bodyshell, the options available to customers could be easily demonstrated. The offside showed the potential for side-mounted sign boards, placed on a flat upper side panel. The lower portion of the offside illustrated the potential for the use of wider wheels, with the inclusion of a glass fibre Traveller rear wing as an add-on component. The nearside had a more traditional profile – a flat panel with a distinctive lower edge, accentuating the line of the wheel arch.

The rear end incorporated a single rear door. This was a two-piece moulding with inner and outer shells. To complete the external features, the prototype used the original-style Traveller rear bumpers and light fittings.

All that was needed was an influx of orders and customers willing to embark on the conversion of their Traveller to a light commercial vehicle. Unfortunately, the project was short-lived, as the hoped-for orders never materialised. Gary Webb, proprietor of the Custom Car Company, was forced to admit that the Travan failed to create the positive response he had anticipated. As a consequence the prototype vehicle was eventually dismantled, and the van back and the associated components were sold to a Morris Minor trader.

The Custom Fibreglass Company advertising literature stressed that it was not simply a kit but a custom built conversion, built around a structurally sound Morris Traveller.

Different options were offered in terms of the rear wheel arch design.

137

The rear GRP section as purchased.

The design was reminiscent of the Danish produced DOMI van which had a single opening rear door and extended roof and side panels.

A new rear frame was fabricated in order to provide additional strength to the rear structure.

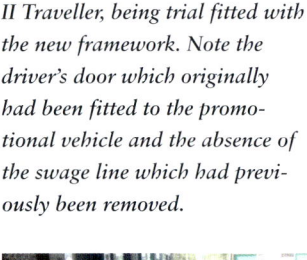

The donor vehicle, a 1955 Series II Traveller, being trial fitted with the new framework. Note the driver's door which originally had been fitted to the promotional vehicle and the absence of the swage line which had previously been removed.

Special provision was made to accommodate the spare wheel in the rear compartment.

RENEWED INTEREST

In 2002, the original prototype van back was acquired by Morris Minor specialist Martin O'Dowd. Experienced in the restoration of early Minors and having owned a number of Series II commercials, Martin was familiar with the Danish DOMI van. Initial thoughts were that the van back could be married up with the front cab of a van or pick-up. However, it soon became apparent that the newly-acquired van back had insufficient inherent strength to be simply bolted to the separate chassis of a commercial. Another limiting factor was that the doors on vans and pick-ups are shorter than on Travellers, and that the back was conceived with the use of longer Traveller doors in mind. It was obvious that a Traveller would have to be sourced in order for the project to progress.

Fortunately help was at hand in the shape of an abandoned restoration project which had been partially stripped. Dating from 1955, a Series II Traveller which had been languishing in a corner of the yard and open to the elements seemed ideal for the project, even though much structural refurbishment would be needed. Documentation proving entitlement to the original registration number UAL 866 and a Heritage Certificate which detailed the original specification including the Empire Green colour, provided sufficient impetus for a start to be made.

Exposure to the elements had done little to preserve the rear floor area, which only had minimal protection from the roof which was still attached, even though all the timber, the windows, and the side panels had been removed. Severe corrosion had set in, in the usual Traveller rot spots, and remedial work had to be done to the rear of the inner wheel arches to strengthen the mounting points. Inside the cab some previous repair work was re-done to a higher professional standard, and some additional work was done to strengthen the inner sills. One of the cross member ends was replaced, and a considerable amount of work was completed at the base of the A-post, a well-known trouble spot. Lots of good, second-hand, bolt-on, external panels were sourced for the rest of the vehicle.

FITTING THE TRAVELLER VAN BACK

This was a major undertaking that required considerable planning and a fair degree of ingenuity. An early decision was taken to extend the boot floor at the rear of the vehicle by four inches, and to create a rear channel at the outer rear edge in order to provide sufficient strength to mount the new structure. Investigation revealed that one of the original ideas was to bond the new body to the original metal structure. On reflection this was deemed to be too problematic, given that there was insufficient strength in the van back. In any case, there was a high risk of flexing which might cause cracks to

COMMERCIAL TRAVELLER CONVERSIONS

appear in the GRP body. In addition it was felt that carrying out any future welding repairs would be difficult to complete with the glass fibre body in situ.

Although there was additional strength built into the structure via the ribbing, particularly in the roof area, the decision was made to increase the rigidity of the structure by adding an in-house designed metal framework. This was made from ¾in thin-wall square-section steel tubing. The simple design followed the outline of the original wooden frame as fitted to the Traveller. It incorporated a wrap-around section adjacent to the inner wheel arches, a ladder section under the rear door, upright supports at each corner, and a waist rail on either side. The frame, which provided much needed rigidity to the whole structure, was fixed to the floor, using some of the original mounting points for the ash frame. However, some new mountings were made at the rear of the wheel arch, and across the back of the vehicle at floor level. Other locating points were the original eight bolt holes on the cab roof panel, and the five bolt holes on the rearward side of each of the door pillars.

An interesting omission in the parts acquired for the conversion was the subframe mentioned in the promotional material. This did not materialise and in consequence, the floor area on the vehicle is lower than that of a normal Traveller. It also accounts for the fact that the spare wheel is not stowed in the usual place under the rear loading platform, as there is insufficient room for it here. Instead a specially-fabricated bracket was constructed, so that the spare could be housed in an upright position on the passenger side of the rear compartment – as it was on the original Minor van.

A further missing item from the specification was the petrol filler flap. Construction and Use regulations insist that this must be recessed beyond the line of the bodywork. So as to avoid falling foul of any regulations, a rectangular hole was cut in the nearside panel in order to fit a plastic housing and a flap from a Volvo 240.

SINGLE DOOR

Like the DOMI van which inspired so much of the project, a single rear door was part of the original concept. The complete door from the prototype was not part of the components acquired. Instead, inner and outer shells were supplied as separate parts to make the door from. After much deliberation, plywood inserts were fixed in place to provide additional strength for the hinges and locking bars that needed to be fitted. The two halves were then bonded together using a commercially bonded epoxy resin, and the cavity was filled with expanding foam. A one-off window was commissioned and made from Lexan, a material with bullet-proof qualities. It was professionally fitted by Auto Windscreens, using a special bonding process. Obtaining a perfect seal on the rear door proved an almost insurmountable challenge, from the point of view of making it both waterproof and rattle-proof. Numerous seals were tried with varying degrees of success.

With the rear section fitted, paintwork was completed in a non-original Morris colour, Spanish Green.

Improved comfort levels, courtesy of adjustable Austin Metro seats, as well as carpets and covered door panels, all added to the individual style of the vehicle.

The opportunity was taken to upgrade the vehicle by fitting a Marina 1275 engine and Marina disc brakes. The rear lights and indicator units came from a VW type 2 Camper van.

As a concept the initial idea had merit. The fact that only two vehicles are known to have been completed, and that the original moulds have been destroyed, means that UAL 866 is unique.

With the back securely mounted and the rigidity substantially increased, all that remained was to add some mouldings to break up the blandness of the van sides. An aluminium moulding was added to provide a swage line from the door handle rearwards. In addition, an aluminium roof guttering, similar to that found on Traveller models, was fitted.

Considerable time and effort was expended on the final paint finish. In spite of copious amounts of two-pack primer and constant flatting down, it was difficult to get rid of the ripple effect on the GRP panels. This prompted the fitting of some Diabond panels to the van sides so that the van could be signwritten. This helped to deflect attention from slight imperfections in the Spanish Green paintwork, and improved the overall appearance of the vehicle.

The essential character of the Series II model was retained by the front end with the original grille and the split windscreen. However, the interior trim and the mechanical specifications differed greatly from those of a standard 1955 Morris Minor Traveller. This Travan, as it became known, was powered by a 1275cc Morris Marina engine mated to a standard 1098cc Minor gearbox. Additional braking power came from Marina disc brakes at the front and Marina 9in (229mm) drum brakes at the rear. Personal preferences dictated the choice of alloy wheels. A specially cast set of Compomotive 14x6J wheels were made, and fitted with 175/65-14 tyres commonly used on Rover 214 Series cars.

The interior trim retained elements of the original specification but comfort levels were increased by fully adjustable Austin Metro seats, which were covered in suede green vinyl. Door cards and other trim parts were covered to match. Other personal adjustments were made to the fascia, with additional instrumentation and contrasting painted panels.

Ironically the completed Travan attracted lots of attention, but by the time the project car was completed in late 2002, the original moulds had been destroyed. One other set of parts are known to exist but UAL 866 remains a unique Morris Minor Traveller. It is now in Southern Ireland, and sports a revised rear door made from aluminium with a moulded spare wheel holder, akin to those seen on Lincoln Continental models.

A Welsh owner fitted a Minor van body to his Traveller around 1990. Because of the longer Traveller front doors, the rear body had to be fitted further back than on the normal van, so the vehicle was longer overall. The lower rear side panels had to be reworked to move the wheel arch further forward in the panel, and had rear wings which were similar in outline to those found on the Traveller.

TRAVELLER PICK-UP

Another UK company which relied heavily on the use of GRP to create an alternative Traveller based vehicle was Wood Brothers. The company, established in 1978, specialised in the buying and selling of Morris Minors. Additional aspects of the business involved servicing and repairs, the supply of replacement parts, and specialist services in respect of welding and woodwork repairs. In a clever marketing ploy to promote the business, Wood Brothers converted a split-screen Woodie into

A specially designed fascia with distinctive magnolia coloured instrumentation including a rare period Smiths clock was added.

COMMERCIAL TRAVELLER CONVERSIONS

The Wood Brothers Traveller Pick-up, complete with GRP tailgate incorporating wood effect panels. A number of kits were purchased in the 1980's and the concept has been replicated with varying degrees of success by individual owners in more recent times.

a pick-up and had the 'new' vehicle appropriately sign-written. Subsequently they produced a kit to enable owners of 'tired Travellers' to give their vehicles a new lease of life, as a stylish mock wood-framed pick-up. Curiously enough, in former years some original pick-ups had been converted to Traveller-like vehicles, with the addition of a top, some times timber-framed.

The kit, which in 1983 was sold for just over £300, comprised a GRP cab back and a one-piece rear body section. The tailgate, which was supplied with all the necessary fittings, was specially moulded to replicate the wood effect on the lower panels of the original rear doors. The half-timbered effect was quite striking, and at the time the conversion attracted considerable interest from small businesses, including window cleaners, builders, and market gardeners. A roll-back tonneau cover helped protect the open back from the elements. An unusual feature of this pick-up was the additional room, and greater ease of access through the longer doors originally fitted to the Traveller. The spare wheel was housed within the cab. A fitting service was provided by the company, but the conversion kit was also provided off the shelf for the enthusiastic owner who wished to tackle the job at home. Rather optimistically, the advertising literature claimed that any competent handyman could complete the conversion in one day!

This late model Traveller has recently undergone a complete restoration to replicate the essential features of the conversion originally carried out in the late 1970s

MORRIS MINOR TRAVELLER – THE COMPLETE COMPANION

Unlike the Wood Brothers conversion, the rear tail gate has an ash frame and a marine ply inner panel.

A RECENTLY RESTORED TRAVELLER PICK-UP

The Wood Brothers concept has lived on, even if the company no longer exists. The fully-restored late model Traveller Pick-up illustrated here certainly wasn't completed in a day. Dating from 1971, it is believed that this particular Traveller Pick-up was commissioned not long after the original Traveller was registered for use on the road. It is thought that the original owner engaged Wood Brothers to create the unique ash frame as a one-off project. The design predates their glass fibre conversions which followed later.

In contrast to the fitting of the Wood Brothers kit in a day, several months and a great deal of planning went into restoring the vehicle seen here. Though faithful to the original design, the finish of many of the components is of a much higher standard. Examples include the carefully designed and constructed, ash-framed rear tail gate which used the rear hinges from a Traveller, the fine detail of the wood-framed rear window, and the inclusion of additional rear side windows to improve visibility. The side frames follow the original pattern, as adopted on the Traveller, and were specially made by Steve Foreman who completed the restoration.

The inner part of the rear load area is fully lined with marine ply, with special boxed-in rear wheel arches. The interior of the cab remains as it was when the vehicle was a Traveller and the spare wheel is carried under the boot well floor, as per the original Traveller design. The overall result is quite stunning, but clearly vehicles like this one are destined to be one-offs. Financial considerations would make any thought of volume production unrealistic, given that Austin and Morris Minor pick-ups were, and are, cheaper and more useable alternatives.

The Traveller pick-up during its rebuild.

CHAPTER 14
MODIFICATIONS AND UPGRADES

The many innovative design features of the original Morris Minor prompted some owners to push the boundaries in terms of performance, handling, and braking. Inspired in part by the quest for more speed, as exemplified in motor sport where the Morris Minor and other marques powered by the reliable A-series engine were commonly seen in the 1950s and 1960s, many owners replicated the upgrades and modifications applied there. Traveller owners were no exception and, in an effort to improve the power to weight ratio, many adopted engine upgrades and transplants. During the production period from 1953 to 1971, a number of options were available.

The expansive engine bay common to all Morris Minor models meant that there was ample room to install a larger engine, for instance in the early Series MM days, the 1200cc ohv engine from the Austin A40 Devon or Somerset, or to add performance enhancing components. Commercial companies provided a number of bolt-on options for the A-series engine. Various tuning options, including some which offered race and rally performance levels, led to impressive results. A considerable number of companies in the UK offered products designed to improve acceleration times and overall top speed for ordinary cars used on the road, particularly those with the A-series engine.

Alexander Engineering based in Buckinghamshire, Powerplus in Gloucestershire, and Speedwell Performance Conversions in London, all endeavoured to improve performance by different levels of engine tuning and improved carburetion. Alexander Engineering raised the compression ratio to 8.9:1. By reshaping and polishing the combustion chambers and ports, adding double valve springs, two 1½in SU carburettors, and including a revised light alloy induction manifold they improved performance markedly, with a top speed of over 80mph (130 km/h) and better acceleration through the gears.

Speedwell Performance Conversions adopted a similar approach. They too used twin SU carburettors, and modified the engine by reshaping the combustion chambers and ports. With reshaped inlet valves, hardened exhaust valves, and specially manufactured valve springs, output in excess of 50bhp was possible. The advantages of fitting the Speedwell conversion were well documented in the motoring press, with claims of halving the 0-60mph acceleration times for the Morris Minor and increasing the top speed by 12mph (19 km/h). More significantly, the power increase in the lower and middle ranges allowed the vehicles to be driven with less stress to the engine, and with improved fuel economy. Speedwell, aware of the need for improvements to the suspension in order to cope with the increased power, also offered rear telescopic shock absorber kits.

Powerplus claimed their conversion improved acceleration and improved top speed to 75mph (121 km/h). They offered a modified cylinder head on an exchange basis, which raised the compression ratio to 8.75:1. The rest of the performance kit included two semi-downdraft SU carburettors, and a three-branch exhaust manifold combined with a straight-through silencer.

Other options included the fitting of superchargers.

Graham Barnes is the proud owner of this highly modified Traveller, finished in gleaming Black paintwork.

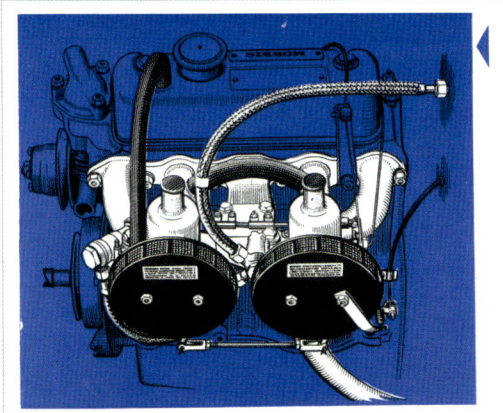

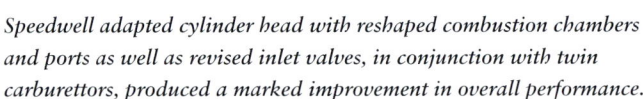

Speedwell adapted cylinder head with reshaped combustion chambers and ports as well as revised inlet valves, in conjunction with twin carburettors, produced a marked improvement in overall performance.

Alexander Engineering advocated the use of twin carburettors as part of their conversion package. In this advertising leaflet, the white portion shows the key components of the engine conversion.

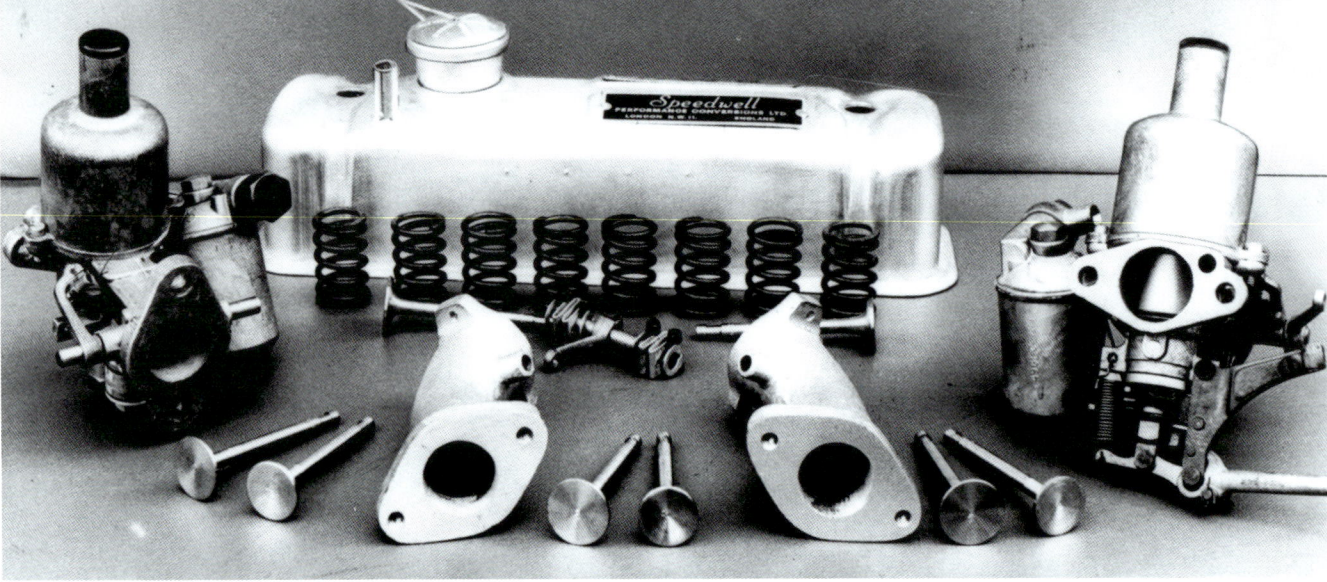

The Shorrock Supercharger. Comprehensive advice and guidance was offered for those wishing to fit the Shorrock Supercharger.

Shorrock and Marshall Nordec were the main suppliers. The Nordec Superchargers were produced by the North Downs Engineering Company Ltd in Caterham, Surrey and marketed variously as the Godfrey Nordec and the Marshall Nordec Superchargers. These were low-pressure superchargers designed to provide a reasonable increase in bhp, but which also aimed to increase engine torque in the lower and middle speed ranges. As such they greatly improved acceleration and hill-climbing, without overstressing the engine. Substantial improvements to acceleration times were claimed, particularly to the 0-60mph time where, for a 948cc engine as fitted to the Morris Minor, an improvement of 10 seconds was recorded.

MODIFICATIONS AND UPGRADES

The Marshall Nordec supercharger. At £92 10s 0d in 1959, the option of fitting a Nordec supercharger did not come cheap, even if the results were impressive for a Morris Minor.

Once fitted, the Nordec supercharger required no additional adjustment or tuning, with routine maintenance being sufficient to ensure smooth running.

Another name synonymous with supercharging, Shorrock, produced a very effective unit for use with the A-series engine. The C75B unit proved a popular and powerful version which when used in the 948cc Morris Minor improved the bhp from the standard 38 to 51, which reduced the 0-60mph time to an impressive 17.4 seconds, and increased the top speed from 72.4mph (116.5 km/h) to 86mph (138.4 km/h). The supercharger enabled at least one-third more fuel than normal to be fed into each cylinder under equal pressure. This in turn produced a greater power output without any significant increase in rpm. A measure of the success of the Shorrock Supercharger is the fact that serviceable examples remain sought-after, decades after production ceased.

THE POST-PRODUCTION ERA

For many enthusiasts the demise of the Morris Minor Traveller in 1971 was premature, even though the economics at the time firmly indicated that producing the Traveller was no longer financially viable. The Morris Marina replaced the Morris Minor and ushered in a new era for British Leyland. With its 1275cc engine, servo-assisted brakes with front discs, and more modern body shape, the Marina and later Ital models had much to commend them. It wasn't long before devotees of the Morris Minor saw the potential for upgrading the performance and stopping power of their now ageing vehicles. Engine transplants from the Marina, together with brake upgrades using the front discs from the same car, along with various gearbox swaps from Ford and Toyota, meant that the potential for the Minor to be used as everyday transport was greatly enhanced.

When I wrote *Morris Minor The First Fifty Years* in 1997, it was not uncommon for Fiat twin-cam engines of up to 2000cc to be fitted in Minors – typically with five-speed gearboxes – and some cars had Ford V4 engines, while in Australia and the USA, Nissan (Datsun) 1200 or 1400cc engines were often fitted, again with five-speed boxes, never mind the more unusual one-off engine transplants. However, it should be noted that while latter-day engine transplants, performance upgrades, and major changes to suspension and brakes, are all perfectly acceptable in the UK (and the USA), they may fall foul of the stricter type approval systems and MOT inspections in other European countries.

MORRIS MINOR WITH 948CC A-SERIES ENGINE, ACCELERATION TIMES

	Standard	Supercharged
0-30mph	7 sec	5.3 sec
0-40mph	11.5 sec	8.2 sec
0-50mph	18.6 sec	12.6 sec
0-60mph	30.3 sec	20.0 sec
0-70mph	n/a	34.5 sec

Once fitted, the Nordec supercharger required no additional adjustment or tuning, with routine maintenance being sufficient to ensure smooth running.

A.D. Engineering completed the development work for what was to become known as the Series III Morris Minor during the 1980s. This is the development car 'WAH'. The Series III concept is still going strong.

A left-hand drive 2012 version of the Series III, bound for Germany.

Improved security with a steering column lock fitted.

THE SERIES III

By the 1980s, Minor specialists such as the Charles Ware Morris Minor Centre at Bath were going even further, and offered upgrades to suspension and interior trim, as well as five-speed gearboxes. In a collaborative venture with AD Engineering an impressive range of upgrades was incorporated into a late-model Morris 1000 Traveller, which for marketing purposes was given the designation Series III. This particular vehicle subsequently became known as the Mighty WAH, a play on the first three letters of the registration mark. Key elements of this vehicle included improved performance from a 1275cc Ital engine, coupled with extensive improvements to suspension and braking.

Essentially the Series III was a pick-and-mix combination of components, designed to suit the pockets of a wide range of customers. The 1275cc Ital engine could be used in standard form, or taken to a higher level of tune. One of the benefits of this engine, which was a further development of the tried and tested A-series, was the flexibility it offered in terms of being able to be mated with relative ease to four-speed gearboxes from Austin-Healey Sprite or MG Midget cars. For those looking for more options, five-speed boxes from the Toyota Corolla and the Ford Sierra could be specified. The Sierra five-speed box was favoured due to its durable nature, the ease with which it could be fitted to the

Marina Disc brakes and uprated suspension.

Anti roll bar for improved handling.

MODIFICATIONS AND UPGRADES

Marina 1300 engine with upgraded ancillaries, including an alternator.

Electric washers are just one of a number of additional upgrades on offer from the Charles Ware Morris Minor Centre to make the Morris Minor Traveller more suited to everyday motoring.

Morris Minor, and the added advantage of having synchromesh on all five forward gears.

Improved braking was achieved by using servo-assisted brakes from the Morris Marina or Ital models. Front disc brakes in combination with larger drum brakes on the rear greatly enhanced the stopping power of the Minor. Another welcome addition was the use of a bulkhead mounted brake fluid reservoir, which increased the brake fluid capacity and thus assisted in providing more efficient use of the disc brakes.

The Series III relied on stronger rear telescopic shock absorbers and new radius arms, to beef up the suspension and combat axle tramp. More recent developments have centred on the front suspension, where the addition of telescopic shock absorbers and an anti-roll bar have dramatically improved road holding and ride. The Series III upgrade package has the advantage of allowing owners the option of retaining the original 14in road wheels. However, it is recommended that 155-14 radial tyres should be used.

The Series III conversion package received universal acclaim in the motoring press when it was first launched.

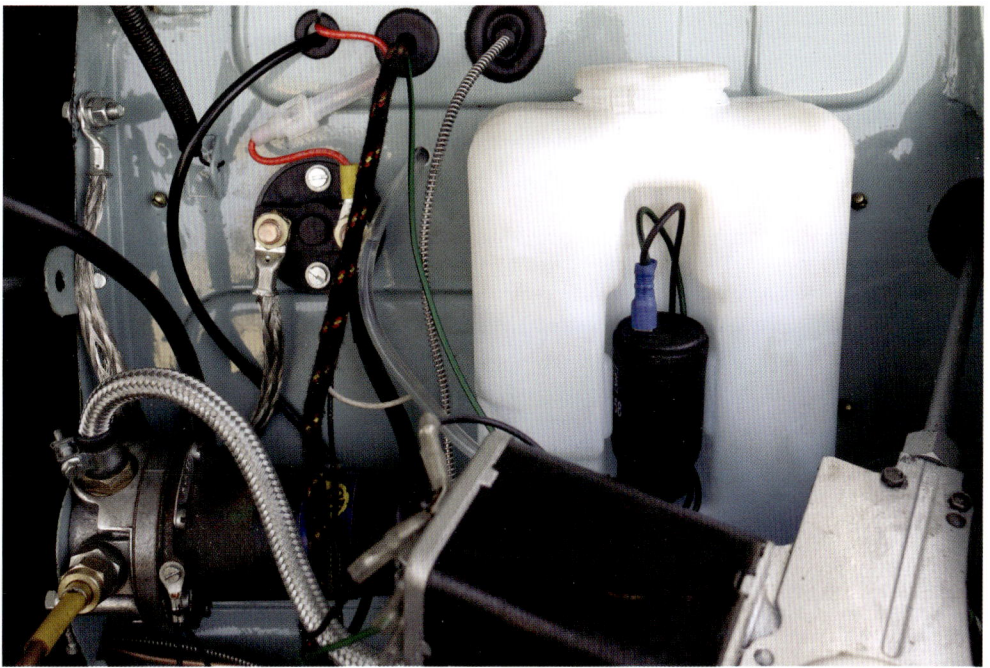

Improved seating in a range of trim combinations are offered as part of the Series III specification

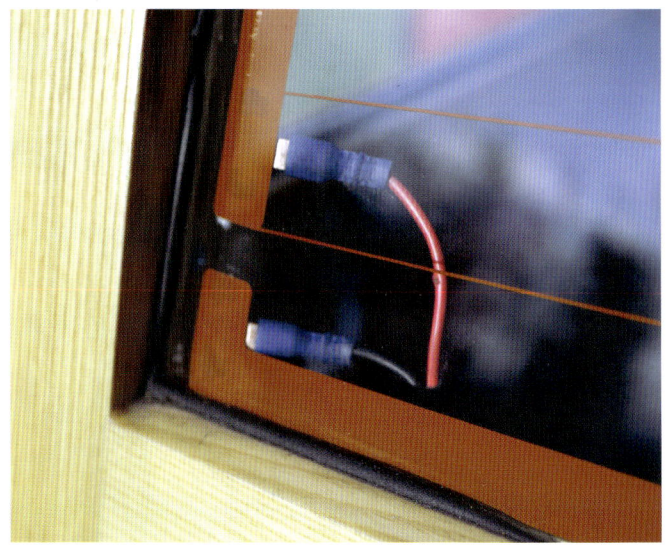

Improved visibility courtesy of a heated rear window.

Autocar tested the Series III in 1985 and did a comparison with the results from their 1964 test of a standard 1098cc Traveller. When tested on the banked track at MIRA, the highest maximum speed on the longest straight was an impressive 90mph (145 km/h) at 5700rpm. The 1275cc A-series engine produced 85bhp at 6000rpm, and tests showed that the acceleration time from 0-60mph through the gears for the Series III was a respectable 17.6 seconds. This represented a 7sec improvement on the figures achieved with the standard 1098cc Traveller in 1964. In terms of handling the verdict was very positive, with credit being given to 'the improved rear axle position, upright telescopic dampers, improved front suspension geometry and the fact that the Series III ran on 4.5 inch wide wheels shod with 175/70R13 tyres'.

Since the 1985 test, the Series III package has been further upgraded, and remains a popular option for owners wishing to improve the comfort and performance of their Morris

MODIFICATIONS AND UPGRADES

The fitting of an automatic gearbox is an option offered as part of the Series III specification.

The gearbox used in the 1300 Morris Marina is the preferred option, for ease of installation with the Marina engine.

Minor Traveller. As well as the mechanical upgrades, improved seating and trim options, better lighting, items such as heated front and rear screens, two-speed wipers, and improved heating and ventilation, are all available to owners wishing to make their Morris Minor a more useable vehicle suited to everyday motoring. A further option is the possibility of fitting an automatic gearbox. The Morris Minor Centre favours the use of the auto box used in the Morris Marina 1300 models.

JLH MODIFICATIONS

Some of the most innovative modification packages currently available have been produced under the direction of Jonathon Heap, proprietor of JLH Minor Restorations Limited. When established in 1993, the company dealt mainly with Morris Minor restorations, but from the outset, mechanical upgrade packages aimed at improving performance were being developed. In the intervening years the effectiveness of a wide range and combination of components and modifications has been assessed, the feasibility of new upgrades appraised, and their suitability for use in the Morris Minor evaluated. Traveller models have featured prominently in the JLH development programme. The Minor's capacity for accommodating modern engines, gearboxes, suspension,

JLH Restorations completed the work on this Traveller which is powered by a Rover K-series engine with a Ford type 9 V6 gearbox and a Ford Escort Mark II rear axle. Power output is 165bhp.

and brakes, has added weight to the long-held view that the original Issigonis concept was well ahead of its time.

JLH pioneered the use of the Rover K-series engine in the Morris Minor. Offered in 1.4, 1.6, and 1.8-litre versions, this lightweight engine, which weighs 16kg less than the original 1098cc A-series, was selected for its excellent reputation for economy, and its potential for further tuning. Even in standard form, the 1.4-litre version produced 120bhp and when mated with a five-speed Ford type 9 gearbox gave a top speed of 120mph (193 km/h). With additional tweaking, it proved possible to increase the power output from the 1.8-litre unit to an impressive 185bhp with a maximum speed of 130mph (209 km/h). With such significant power outputs available, additional braking and suspension modifications were necessary.

The preferred option to improve braking was to use the disc brakes from the Ford Escort Mark III. Incorporated into the modifications were a modified master cylinder kit with bulkhead-mounted reservoir and a brake servo. Most customers opted for disc brakes on the front, with larger diameter drum brakes on the rear. To complete the upgrade, the suspension components needed to be reviewed. In the original specification, the torsion bar independent front suspension was subject to considerable praise. In spite of this, the additional power output demanded that revisions be made to the original set up. JLH chose to offer a number of permutations to cope with the additional power output. Fundamental to the improvements was a change to the rear axle. The original Morris Minor rear axle was no longer an option, so the Ford Escort Mark II axle was added. This offered a greater range of differential ratios, as well as the option to use Ford Capri 9in (229mm) drum brakes, or disc brakes.

Modifying and strengthening the suspension was achieved in a number of ways, some of which required the addition of strengthening brackets and plates, and others which involved structural changes to the rear floor area of the original monocoque construction. The main components used by JLH include fully adjustable telescopic Avo gas dampers, which are mounted on a modified bottom suspension arm which has a lower mounting pin welded to it. New top brackets which considerably strengthen the upper mounting points are made of 3mm steel plate. At the rear, Avo telescopic shock absorbers are used with both axle options. A unique feature of the system is the use of turreted dampers set into the rear floor. This addition allows for the use of wider wheels and keeps all the components within the 'chassis' of the vehicle, and furthermore, is non-intrusive into the load area.

To assist in the elimination of axle tramp, which was a problem which beset the Minor even in standard form, specially-designed triangulated radius arms are fitted to specially strengthened mounting points. A further option designed to improve the front suspension geometry involves fitting adjustable tie bars fitted with poly bushes. These additions significantly improve the ride, comfort and handling of the vehicle, particularly in 'power down' mode, a fact verified and confirmed in numerous road tests and at track events.

Development work is on-going to improve the suspension further, particularly for use on highly-modified vehicles with high levels of performance. The thought of dispensing with the Morris Minor torsion bars, so favoured by Issigonis and his suspension expert Jack Daniels, may seem a step too far for die-hard enthusiasts. Nevertheless, in the interest of progress and in an attempt to push the boundaries still further, JLH have marketed an advanced modification kit for both the front and rear suspension.

The front Coil-Over kit uses coil suspension units and wide lower A arms which replace the original torsion bars, suspension arms, and tie rods. The kit is used in conjunction with the original kingpins, trunnions, and lever arm dampers.

Additional specifications include JLH five-link rear suspension, with JLH front coil-overs, and improved braking by way of a RS Turbo JLH Disc kit and servo.

However, the dampers are only used as a pivotal point. The removal of the torsion bars allows much greater freedom of adjustment on the front suspension geometry. Extra strength and rigidity is provided by the addition of a cross member between the front chassis legs. Elsewhere, welded-on chassis brackets and other strengthening points provide the necessary structure to allow for a fully adjustable front suspension system, which has the potential for changing ride height and damper rate.

To complement this radical change to the front suspension, a five-link kit has been developed for use on the rear suspension, provided a Ford Escort Mark II rear axle is used. When fitted, the components allow for adjustment to ride height, damping control, and differential setting, as well as rear axle and four-wheel alignment. Given the technical nature of the adjustments necessary to gain optimum performance and ride, it is recommended that the setting up is undertaken by qualified and experienced mechanics.

The 2.0 litre Ford Zetec engine is a popular option and fits neatly into the Morris Minor engine bay, with slight modifications to the bulkhead. Four versions of the Zetec are offered by JLH, providing options in power output of 170bhp, 200bhp, 220bhp, and 340bhp supercharged.

Although the K-series engines continue to provide a range of options for Traveller owners wishing to upgrade, new developments continue apace. Anxious to be at the forefront of innovative ideas for alternative power sources for the Morris Minor range, JLH have been promoting the use of the Ford Zetec 2-litre engine.

According to Jonathon Heap, the 2-litre Zetec motor has in effect become the modern-day equivalent of the Fiat twin-cam engine, particularly when considering initial cost, tuning ability, and relative ease of fitting. Though slightly heavier than the K-series, the Zetec has an excellent reliability record. Zetec-powered Minors have the capacity to produce breath-taking performance figures and mind-blowing top speeds: 0-60mph in 5.5 seconds from the 170bhp engine and 0-60mph in 4.5 seconds or less from the 220bhp supercharged version, with a top speed in excess of 135mph (217 km/h) for both, are truly amazing figures for a vehicle which has its roots in the 1940s.

Ever keen to push the boundaries, JLH have explored a variety of gearbox options for use with the Zetec engines. The Ford type 9 gearbox, as used in rear-wheel drive models such as the Sierra, fits directly on to the Zetec engine, but with increasing power outputs being actively considered, JLH have developed a new bellhousing for use in the Morris Minor which will allow the fitting of a Ford T5 Cosworth gearbox, as used in the Ford Cosworth Sierra. In addition, Ford type 9 derived six-speed gearboxes and sequential units are offered as alternatives. Looking to the future, plans are already in hand to incorporate the latest generation of Ford engines into the Morris Minor. The 1.6-litre Ford Sigma VVC engine and the 1.6-litre Ecoboost engine, which is a turbocharged version of the Sigma with a power output of 148-400bhp, are already under consideration.

With the massive power increase and the need for improved suspension, modifications are necessary to the body structure as shown here.

MORRIS MINOR TRAVELLER – THE COMPLETE COMPANION

Along with the performance modifications, it is essential to up-rate the brakes and suspensions systems on the Morris Minor. However it is also important to improve the seating, seat belt provision, and pay attention to the wheels and tyres fitted.

15 inch alloy wheels with 195/55/15 high-performance tyres are favoured by JLH. Here Peugeot 205 GTI alloys have been selected.

Finishing touches include a wood-rimmed steering wheel and an Aero style filler cap.

Interior modifications on offer include a redesigned fascia panel 40mm wider than the original, which results in shorter glove boxes. It incorporates a new style 130mph speedometer.

Though JLH tend to concentrate on bodywork and the mechanical aspects of modifying and upgrading the Morris Minor, other improvement options form part of the company portfolio. Whether it be custom-made glass fibre panels, tinted windows, upgraded seats, two-speed wipers, a heated front screen, heated rear windows, a more powerful and more efficient heater, or a redesigned dashboard with a bespoke centrepiece with additional dials, all can be incorporated.

The continued interest in the Morris Traveller, and the desire for them to be used as everyday vehicles, has created a demand for improving interior comfort. The original Morris Minor seats, while adequate when the cars were in production, fall well short of modern-day expectations. Comfort in terms of lumbar support, back rest adjustment, and seat positioning, is sadly lacking. Not surprisingly, many Traveller owners have forsaken originality in favour of improved comfort and posture. Specialist suppliers have risen to the challenge and provided a number of options. New seat mounting bases, with runners on which seats from a variety of vehicles can be mounted, have proved popular. Front seats from the Austin Metro were a favourite at one time, but these have been superseded by the seats from the MGF. Classic car trim specialists Newton Commercial offer MGF type seats which they call Suffolk seats, trimmed to tone in with the rest of the Morris Minor interior. The Morris Minor Centre of Bath offer modern seats trimmed in either vinyl or a half-hide leather option, and even offer a modern version of the early 1960s duo-tone upholstery, while JLH offer a bespoke service, based on customer requirements.

Other aspects of modernising the Traveller for use in the twenty-first century include installing halogen headlights, reversing lights, hazard warning lights, side indicator repeaters on the front wings, and making provision for modern technology, such as the installation of combined radio and CD players, and MP3, mobile phone, and iPod docking stations. Such additions will necessitate the fitting of an alternator for its increased output, if one has not been previously installed.

With such a wealth of tried and tested options available, the future looks bright for the Morris Minor Traveller owner. An added bonus is the fact that even when modified, the essential character of the original Morris Traveller remains unchanged. For some enthusiasts, the restored and up-rated Traveller presents a vision of how things might have been, had the Morris Minor remained in production.

As the Morris Minor Traveller heads past the sixty-year mark since it entered production, it will be interesting to see what future developments there may be, particularly as environmental pressures increase, the need for alternative fuels will have to be accommodated, and changes in legislation considered. The days of the Diesel-hybrid Traveller may not be too far away.

APPENDIX
THE NUMBERS EXPLAINED

There were two types of chassis number prefixes found on Minor Travellers.

From 1953 to 1958, a Nuffield system was used with a five (later four) character prefix which may be read as follows:
First letter **F** for Morris Minor
Second letter **L** for Traveller body
Third letter for colour,
for instance **A** for black, **B** for grey, **C** for red, **D** for blue, **E** for green, and **F** for beige (other letters may be found on later cars)
First number for specification class, **1** for RHD home, **2** for RHD export, **3** for LHD, **4** for LHD North America, **5** for CKD RHD, and **6** for CKD LHD
Second number for type of paint finish (omitted from January 1958), typically **1** for synthetic

From 1958 to 1971, the BMC prefix system was used:
First letter **M** for Morris
Second letter **A** for engine smaller than 1200cc
Third letter **W** for Traveller body
Followed by a number for series, either **3** on 948cc engined cars or **5** on 1098cc engined cars
There may be one or two extra letters, **L** for Left-hand drive, and **D** for De Luxe

From the autumn of 1967 onwards, chassis numbers were suffixed with a letter indicating assembly plant, **M** for Morris at Cowley or **F** for Adderley Park (**G** was for MG at Abingdon)

Chassis numbers were issued in the series of numbers which was used for all Minor cars (but not LCV models) and which had commenced with **501** in 1948.

TRAVELLER CHASSIS NUMBER SEQUENCE:

1953, 30 September	First Traveller	216901
1954	First in year	233718
1955	First in year	307208
1956	First in year	395987
1956, 25 September	First Minor 1000 948cc	448801
1957	First in year	464995
1958	First in year	569667
1958, 29 October	New style chassis prefix	660601
1959	First in year	683433
1960	First in year	790007
1961	First in year	886161
1962	First in year	946761
1962, 17 September	First Minor 1098cc	990290
1963	First in year	1005483
1964	First in year	1051386
1965	First in year	1092770
1966	First in year	1131829
1967	First in year	1170439
1968	First in year	1208361
1969	First in year	1241050
1969, 18 July	Last Cowley-built	1257425
1969	Adderley Park built from	1261201
1970	First in year	1268276
1971	First in year	1290813
1971, April	Last Traveller	1294082

Note that all first in year numbers quoted are approximate. Slightly different numbers are some times quoted, for instance in *Glass's Car Check Book*. The numbers quoted here are based on the original production ledgers held in the archive of the Heritage Motor Centre at Gaydon, from where Morris Minor owners can obtain a certificate giving the exact details of their car, except for Adderley Park-built vehicles since those records are presumed to have been destroyed. Chassis numbers for Adderley Park built Travellers were in distinct batches of numbers allocated out of the main sequence of numbers. More detailed lists of change points may be found in the author's companion volume *Original Morris Minor*, also published by Herridge and Sons.

APPENDIX: THE NUMBERS EXPLAINED

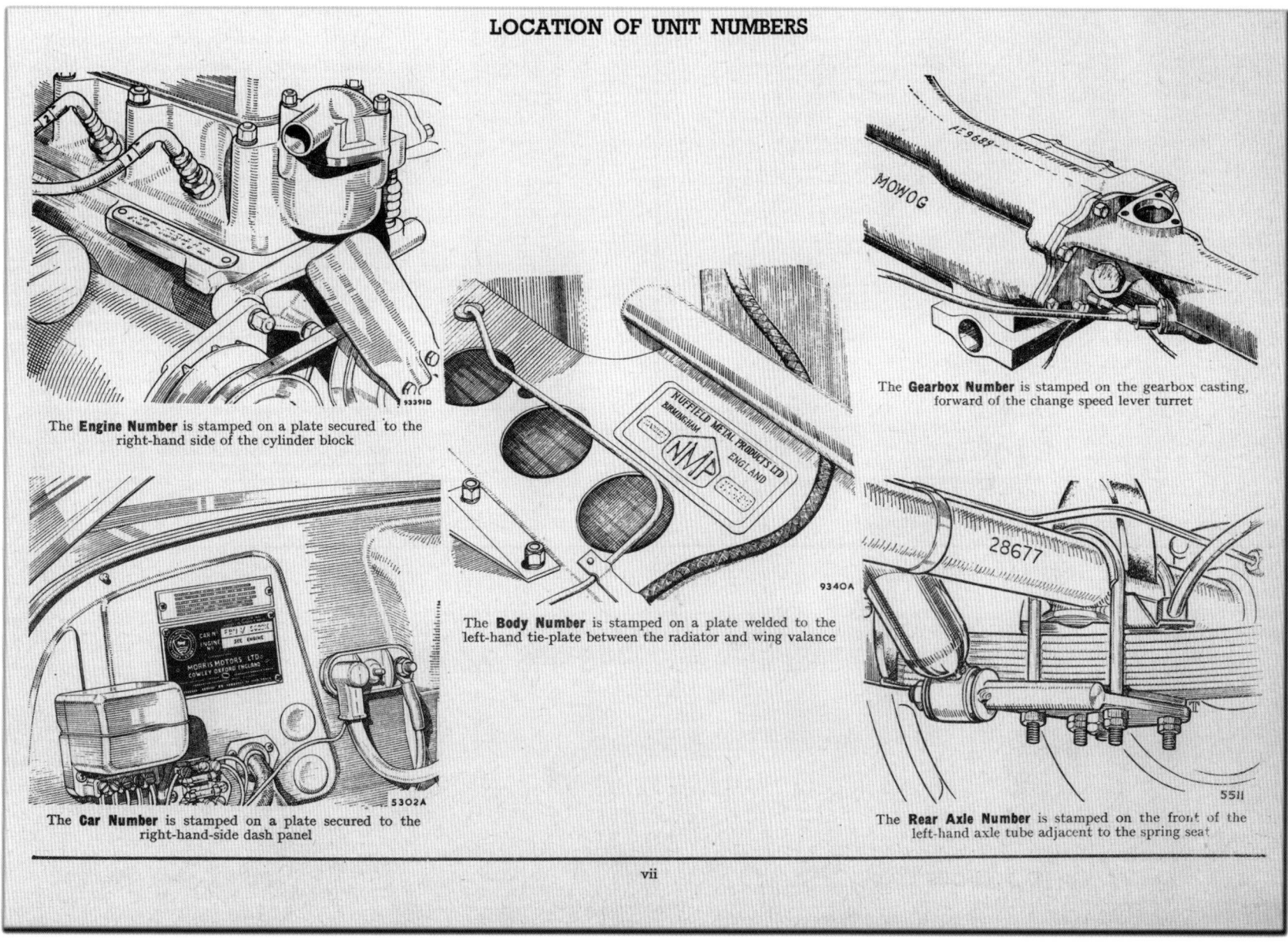

ENGINE NUMBERS

Each engine type had its own sequence of numbers often commencing with **101**. The following different prefixes were found:

APHM: Series II 803cc, 1953-56
APJM: Minor 1000 948 cc, 1956-57
9M-U-H (or 9M-U-L): Minor 1000 948cc, 1957-62
10MA-U-H (or 10MA-U-L): Minor 1000 1098cc, 1962-69
10ME-U-H: 1098cc with positive crankcase ventilation for the USA, ca. 1963-67
10V-189-E-H (or -L): Minor 1000 1098cc, from March 1969
10V-190-E-H (or -L): ditto, if fitted with alternator

On engines from 1957 to 1969, 9 or 10 indicates capacity, M indicates Morris, A or E is for variant, U is for remote centre gear change, and H or L is for High or Low compression ratio. On the final engines, V is for 'Vertical' installation for rear-wheel drive, the three-digit code number indicates detailed specification, and the final letter is again for compression.

BODY NUMBERS

Each Traveller had one or two body numbers which were often found on separate tags on the bulkhead behind the engine, with letter prefixes, either **Z** which seems to be common to Minors generally, or **BMD** which is unique to the Traveller.

The BMD body numbers are usually recorded, without prefix, in the ledgers found at Gaydon. The body number series in the ledgers started with the number **501** in 1953, and these body numbers continued in the same series to the end of production; the body numbers are therefore to some extent an indication of production figures, although it is uncertain whether all CKD cars had body numbers allocated.

By the time of introduction of the Minor 1000 in 1956, the body numbers had reached around 21,000 in the ledgers, suggesting a production figures of approximately 20,500 Series II Travellers over a three-year period.

In 1969 when production was transferred from Cowley to Adderley Park, the body number series in the ledgers had reached approximately 205,100, suggesting a total Cowley (and Abingdon) production of say 204,600 Travellers. Comparing with the annual production figures (see chapter 5) this suggests there were over 15,000 Travellers built at Adderley Park in the final two years of production.

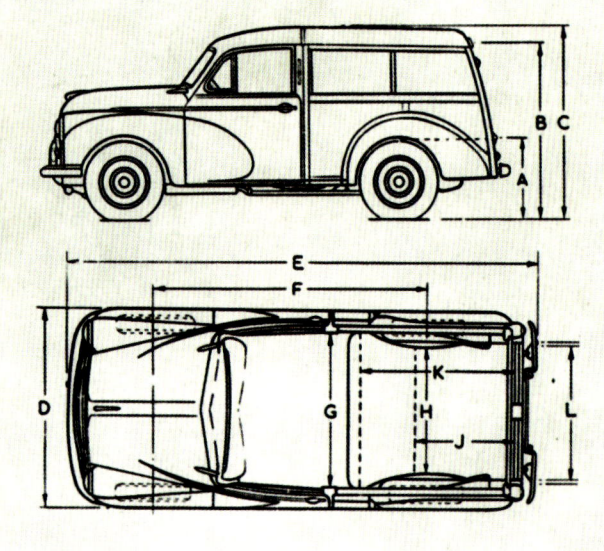

MINOR TRAVELLER

A 26½ in. 67 cm. (unladen)	**B** 55½ in. 141 cm.	**C** 60½ in. 154 cm.
D 61 in. 155 cm.	**E** 149 in. 378 cm.	**F** 86 in. 218 cm.
G 46½ in. 118 cm.	**H** 39 in. 99 cm.	**J*** 31 in. 79 cm.
K† 50 in. 127 cm.	**L** 41 in. 104 cm.	

* At floor level with rear seat in position.
† At floor level with rear seat folded.

ACKNOWLEDGMENTS

Putting together the material for this title would not have been possible without the assistance of a considerable number of people, all of whom have willingly given of their time and knowledge to provide photographs or to reaffirm factual information on the Morris Minor Traveller and other related models. I am indebted to them all, especially Morris Minor Owners Club members Sandy and Rosie Hamilton, Bryan Gostling, Stephen Morris, Kevin Daly, Alan Scott, Tim Heenan, Ashley Holmes, Dave Walker and Sam McAfee. Club Registrars Gerry Cambridge and Simon Mitchell have been unstinting in their quest for accuracy in relation to Military Travellers and Police vehicles as have owners David Price, Lesley Price and Drew Edwards. Former Panda Register Registrar Roger Tennyson's assistance has been invaluable, particularly in sourcing photographic material relating to Police and Military Police vehicles.

Once again photographer John Colley has excelled in providing images for many of the chapters in this book. Specific photographs have been taken for this publication and these, along with many archive pictures previously taken by John, help to accurately record the original specifications and features of the various Traveller models. I am grateful to the many owners who provided their vehicles for various photo shoots. In particular, John Hales and Marcus Ward who braved the elements in Derbyshire, Brian Wood, Ron Tickner and Phil Traves who sought out various locations in Dorset, and Keith Lyall who patiently photographed his wife's recently restored Traveller in Worcestershire. Special thanks must also go to Leo Greenway who provided the rare black and white images of the glass fibre framed Traveller from his own collection.

The Morris Minor Traveller story would not be complete without specific reference to its predecessor the Morris Oxford Travellers Car. Morris Oxford and Wolseley 6/80 Club members and officials have been very supportive, none more so than MO Traveller owners Bruce Henderson and Ian Biltcliffe. The content relating to the Morris Oxford Traveller has been considerably enhanced by the photographs of Ian's Traveller and the contemporary materials which he kindly supplied.

The Morris Minor Traveller was a popular model in overseas markets and in seeking to do justice to exported models, overseas variants and CKD models I sought and received considerable assistance from fellow enthusiasts in Holland, Denmark, South Africa, Australia and America. In Holland Jan Sol, Evert Spape, Anton Visser and Rimmo Gritter researched information on CKD and BAOR Travellers and supplied photographic and factual information. In Denmark, Simon Marsboll tracked down and photographed rare surviving Combi models and helped unravel the intricacies of the Danish tax and registration systems as they related to Morris Minor Combi and Super Combi models. Additional verification was added by Niels Jonassen of the Danish Veteran Car Club. Elsewhere special arrangements were made to photograph South African assembled Morris Minor Travellers at the 2012 National Rally in Port Elizabeth, as well as a rare Traveller located in Melbourne Australia owned by Richard McKellar. In America Tony Burgess and Randolf Williams sourced valuable information on individual vehicles and advised on the export of Morris Minors to the USA.

The Morris Minor is one of the most enduring and popular classic cars, and in the UK in particular there is a comprehensive network of traders who provide a range of services, parts and upgrades, thus ensuring the continued use and preservation of the vehicles. Many traders have assisted with specific information and photographic images. Martin O'Dowd (Retro Autos), Tim Brennan and Zac Ware (Charles Ware Morris Minor Centre), Jonathan Heap (JLH Restorations), Rick Bowers (Ace Classic Cars) and Andrew Bywater (Morris Minor Hearse Company) have all been extremely helpful, patient and generous with their valuable time in dealing with my frequent requests for clarification.

My research has been greatly assisted by staff at the Heritage Motor Centre, particularly by Jan Valentino in the Archive Department, as well as by Michelle Worthington at RAF Cosford, who kindly arranged for photographs to be taken of the ex-Army Traveller displayed there. Mark Watkins has also assisted greatly in providing technical back-up with scanning of rare images.

A key element of this book is the inclusion of a comprehensive guide to maintaining and replacing Traveller wood. Working with Steve and James Foreman to produce a fully illustrated guide has been a pleasure. For both Steve and me it also represents a real sense of achievement as the publication of this book sees the completion of a project we first talked about over twenty years ago!

Of course none of this would have been possible without the encouragement and support of Charles and Ed Herridge at Herridge and Sons Ltd who have seen the project through to completion. With the additional support and expertise of Anders Clausager, who not only edited the text but added to it with his considerable knowledge, particularly in relation to facts, figures and statistical information, accuracy has been enhanced and quality assured.

My thanks to all who have contributed in any to the creation of this title and to those, especially my wife Susan, who have supported and encouraged me throughout.

Ray Newell.

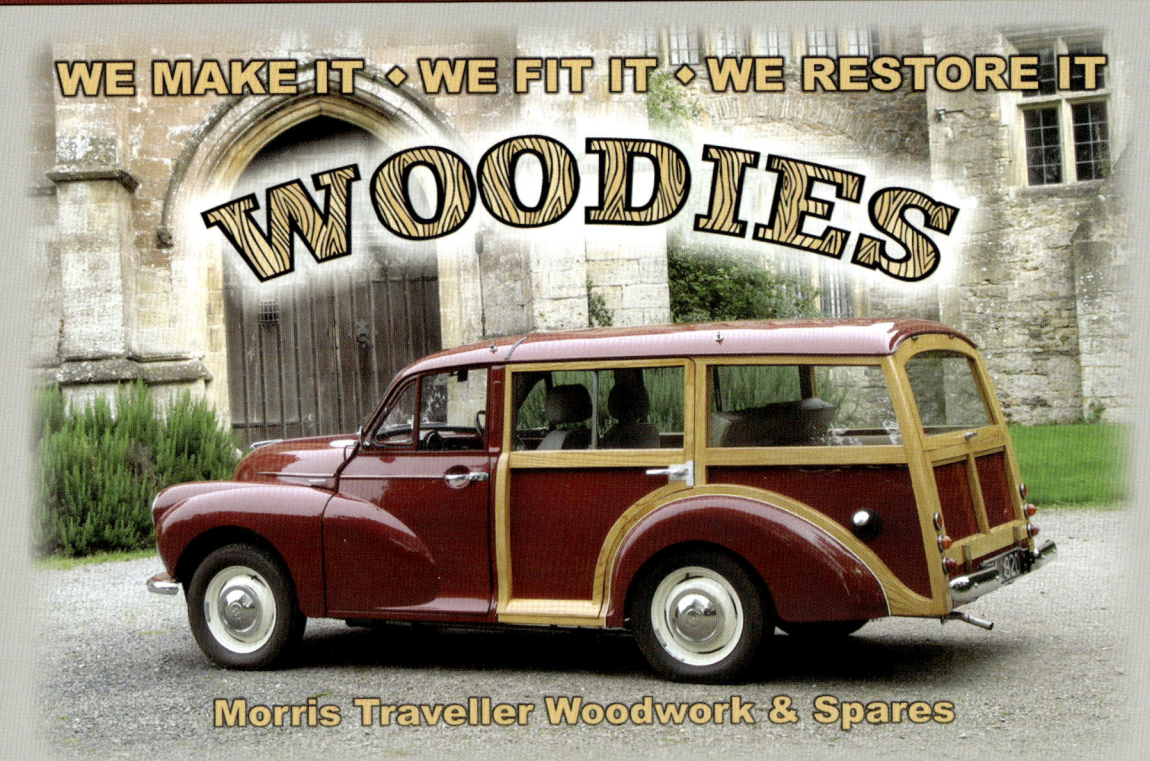

WE MAKE IT • WE FIT IT • WE RESTORE IT
WOODIES
Morris Traveller Woodwork & Spares

For nearly 30 years we have been manufacturing and fitting wood frames to the Morris Traveller, Mini Countryman and various classic and vintage cars. Our experience has shown that the quality of the ash timber is extremely important to the appearance and durability of the frames. We only use slow grown top spec Ash and due to the quantity we buy it in we can colour and grain match all our kits.

As specialists in the Morris Traveller we can undertake pretty much any work your car may need from wood replacement to complete nut and bolt restorations.

We can also supply and fit a whole range of mechanical upgrades to keep your car motoring well into the 21st century!

- **Woodwork Restoration to the Highest Standard**
- **Ash Frames for all Classic and Vintage Vehicles**
- **Recognised Worldwide for our Quality and Service**
- **Customised Woodwork No Problem**

Complete woodkits available for mail order to the UK and for export. Kits include all trims, fixings and instructions.

Ask for Steve or James Foreman for advice, package prices or our fitting service.

www.morriswoodwork.co.uk
tel: 01243 788660 - email: forwoodies@aol.com

Woodies, Unit 25 Eastmead Industrial Estate, Lavant, Chichester, West Sussex, PO18 0DB